QuikFind

**Topical Categories
from your Bible Paraphrased**

Compiled By **Bruce G. Conley**

AMBASSADOR
EMERALD INTERNATIONAL

Greenville, South Carolina • Belfast, Northern Ireland
www.emeraldhouse.com

Quick FInd
© 2002 Bruce G. Conley

Scripture refrences are from the King James Version

Ambassador Emerald International
427 Wade Hampton Boulevard
Greenville, S.C. 29609 U.S.A.

and

Ambassador Productions Ltd.
Providence House
Ardenlee Street
Belfast BT6 8QJ, Northern Ireland

www.emeraldhouse.com

cover design and page layout by A & E Media, Sam Laterza

ISBN 1 889893 89 7

Acknowledgments

I am deeply indebted to my pastor, Dr. Tom Carter, an author of many Christian books himself, who carefully and professionally edited this book; and to Jeanie Justesen, who helped type the first draft of the manuscript for this book. My special thanks goes to these two people.

In addition, I am grateful to the following friends who, after reading my drafts of this book, gave me valuable feedback and input:

Pastor Armando Alvarado

Pastor Larry Briney

Dr. Tom Carter

Don Fillmore

Lee and Dorothy Halverstadt

Jerry and Jeanie Justesen

Mark Potthoff

Pastor Bill Ragsdale

Norman Rohrer

Alphabetical List
of Topics

INTRODUCTION

For thirty years I wrote selected Bible verses with paraphrasing into the front and back pages of my Bible. These
verses were derived from sermons I heard, Sunday school
classes I attended, and Bible study groups I participated in.
Eventually all of the blank pages in my Bible became filled
with verses and paraphrasing.

Unfortunately, I had not written these verses in an organized order, so quick and easy usage became time consum-
ing. In addition, the limited number of verses that I had
written in my Bible were just a sampling of what I believed
was desirable.

I felt awkward carrying both my Bible and a concordance
to church, Sunday school, or my Bible study group. Of
course some Bibles have a built-in concordance, but they
exclude many verses, so that didn't satisfy me, either.

In January of 1998, I committed to reading my Bible a
minimum of one hour—sometimes longer—each day. I
found it fascinating and began writing down specific verses
that were among the most popular in the Bible. I paraphrased these popular verses and combined them with the
selected few verses that I had written in the front and back
of my Bible. To keep myself spiritually fresh, I read several
different versions of the Bible.

The results were seventy-four cards that I clipped together and carried in the back of my Bible. I organized them into alphabetical categories such as: *abortion, apostle, death, heaven, hell, homosexuality* (try to find this word in a concordance), *horoscope, marriage, money, resurrection, salvation, witnessing*, and many others.

During the summer and fall of 2000 I casually began to share with a few people what I had been doing. They became excited and asked me how they could secure a copy. At first I discounted their enthusiasm until finally enough people stressed that they wanted and needed something like this for themselves, their families, and their friends.

This awakened me to the felt need of many people for an easy and fast approach to the Bible. Thus I have written this book that paraphrases 1635 of the most popular verses in the Bible and arranges them into ninety-four topics. The verses in each topic are listed sequentially in the order of Bible appearance.

I offer *QuikFind* as a simple bridge between you and your Bible. May the quick and easy access that it provides into God's wonderful Word bring you into a deeper knowledge of the Lord it proclaims.

Bruce G. Conley

ABORTION

Genesis 9:6 . . . . .Shedding the blood of man by man shall result in his blood being shed.

Exodus 21:22-25 . . . . . . .Whoever causes the death or injury of an unborn baby must be punished—an eye for an eye, a tooth for a tooth, a hand for a hand, a burn for a burn, etc.

Psalm 51:5 . . . . .King David states that he is a sinner from the time his mother conceives him (unborn children are persons and sinners from the time they are conceived).

Psalm 139:13 . . . . .God creates my inmost being. He knit me together in my mother's womb.

Proverbs 31:8 . . . . .speak up for those who cannot speak for themselves, for the rights of all who are destitute.

Isaiah 44:2 . . . . .The Lord makes you and forms you in the womb.

Jeremiah 1:5 . . . . .God tells Jeremiah that He knew him before he was in the womb.

Luke 1:41-44 . . . . .Elizabeth's baby leaps for joy in her womb (the unborn baby has a mind).

1 Corinthians 3:16-17 . . .Don't you know that you are God's temple and that God's Spirit lives in you? If anyone destroys God's temple, God will destroy him.

1 Corinthians 6:19-20 . . .Your body is not your own.
Honor God with your body.

ADULTERY

Leviticus 20:10 . . . . . . .If a man commits adultery with
another man's wife, both the
adulterer and the adulteress must
be put to death.

2 Samuel 11:1-17 . . . . . .King David commits lust and
adultery with Bathsheba and has
her husband, Uriah, murdered.

Job 31:1 . . . . .Make a covenant with your eyes
not to look lustfully at a girl.

Psalm 51:12 . . . . .After King David commits adultery with Bathsheba, he asks
God to restore in him the joy of
salvation and grant him a willing
spirit to sustain him.

Matthew 5:27-28 . . . . . . .Do not commit adultery. Anyone
who looks at a woman lustfully
has already committed adultery
with her in his heart (See
Matthew 5:32).

Mark 10:11-12 . . . . .If you divorce your spouse and
marry someone else, you com-
mit adultery.

Romans 13:9 . . . . .The commandment, "Do not
commit adultery."

1 Corinthians 6:9-10 . . . .Neither the wicked, the sexually
immoral, idolaters, adulterers,
male prostitutes, nor homosexual

offenders will inherit the kingdom of God.

APOSTASY (FALLING AWAY)

Exodus 32:1 . . . . .When Moses is gone, the
Israelites worship other gods.

Judges 2:16-17 . . . . .The Lord raises up judges who
save the Israelites from their
enemies, yet the Israelites worship other gods.

Nehemiah 9:26 . . . . .The Israelites are disobedient
and rebel against the Lord. They
kill the Lord's prophets.

Psalm 2:1-3 . . . . .The kings and rulers gather
together against the Lord.

Matthew 24:6-14 . . . . . . .In the end times many will turn
away from the faith and betray
and hate each other. False
prophets will appear.

Luke 8:13 . . . . .The seed (God's Word) that falls
on rocks (hard hearts) have no
root and in time of testing fall
away.

1 Timothy 4:1 . . . . .In the later times some will
abandon the faith and follow
deceiving spirits and things
taught by demons.

2 Timothy 4:3-4 . . . . .The time will come when men
will not put up with sound doc-
trine. They will turn their ears
away from the truths and turn
aside to myths.

2 Timothy 4:10 . . . . .Because Demas and others so love the world, they desert the apostle Paul.

Hebrews 3:12 . . . . .Do not have a sinful, unbelieving heart that turns away from the living God.

1 John 2:18-19 . . . . .Unbelievers will fall away.

APOSTLES

Matthew 4:18-19 . . . . . .Jesus sees two brothers, Simon called Peter and Andrew, who are fishermen. Jesus says, "Follow me, and I will make you fishers of men."

Matthew 10:1 . . . . .Jesus gives His twelve disciples the power to heal every disease and to drive out evil spirits.

Matthew 10:2-4 . . . . . . .The twelve apostles are Simon Peter, Andrew, James (the son of Zebedee), John, Philip, Bartholomew, Thomas, Matthew, James (the son of Alphaeus), Thaddaeus, Simon the Zealot, and Judas Iscariot, who betrays Jesus (see Luke 6:13-16).

Matthew 10:5-10 . . . . . .Jesus' instructions to the apostles. Do not go among the Gentiles.

Matthew 16:13-17 . . . . . . God reveals to Peter that Jesus is the Christ, the Son of the living God.

Matthew 16:18 . . . . .Jesus tells Peter (whose name means rock), "You are Peter, and upon this rock (his faith and confession in Jesus Christ) I will build my church, and the gates of hell will not overcome it."

Matthew 26:23-25 . . . . . .Jesus predicts His betrayal by Judas Iscariot (see John 13:21-30).

Mark 16:17-18 . . . . .The disciples will pick up snakes with their hands. When they drink deadly poison, it will not hurt them. They will place their hands on the sick people, and they will get well.

Luke 5:1-11 . . . . .The calling of the first disciples. Jesus provides a large catch of fish for Simon Peter, who confesses that he is a sinner. Jesus says, "Don't be afraid. From now on you will catch men."

Luke 22:36 . . . . .Jesus instructs His apostles to sell their coats to buy a sword.

Luke 22:49-50 . . . . .One of the apostles cuts off the ear a servant of the high priest.

Luke 22:51 . . . . .Jesus restores the ear cut off by the sword of the apostle (see John 18:10. Peter cut the right ear off Malchus, the servant of the high priest).

Luke 22:55-62 . . . . .Three times Peter denies knowing Jesus. Then the rooster
crows as predicted.

John 20:24-29 . . . . .Doubting Thomas believes in
Jesus, the Son of God.

Acts 1:23-26 . . . . .Matthias is chosen by drawing
lots (chosen by the Lord) to
replace Judas Iscariot as an
apostle.

Acts 4:13 . . . . .Peter and John are unschooled,
ordinary men.

Acts 12:5-11 . . . . .An angel rescues Peter from
prison.

Galatians 2:7 . . . . .Peter was given the task of
preaching the gospel to the Jews
and Paul the task of preaching
the gospel to the Gentiles.

Revelation 1:10-20 . . . . .Apostle John wrote the book of
Revelation to the seven churches
of Asia. John is in the Spirit and
Christ talks to him as John
observes spiritual surroundings.

ARK OF THE COVENANT

Exodus 25:10-22 . . . . . . .Creating the Ark of the
Covenant, a portable sanctuary
for God, made of acacia wood.
It is forty-five inches long, twen-
ty-seven inches wide, and twen-
ty-seven inches high. (See
Exodus 37:1).

Deuteronomy 10:1-5 . . . .The stone tablets on which the Ten Commandments are written are put into the Ark of acacia wood.

1 Samuel 4:10-11, 21-22 . .The Philistines capture the Ark of the Covenant from Israel.

1 Samuel 5:1-5 . . . . .The statue of Dagon, the god of the Philistines, falls on its face before the Ark of the Covenant, which the Philistines have captured.

1 Samuel 6:19-20 . . . . . .God kills seventy Hebrews for looking into the Ark of the Covenant when the Philistines return it.

1 Kings 8:1-8 . . . . .King Solomon has the Ark put into the Most Holy Place in the temple.

1 Kings 8:9 . . . . .The Ark no longer contains Aaron's staff and jar of manna but still contains the two stone tablets that Moses has placed in it at Horeb.

Hebrews 9:4 . . . . .The initial contents of the Ark of the Covenant are a gold jar of manna, Aaron's rod that has budded, and the stone tablets of the Ten Commandments.

Revelation 11:19 . . . . . . .Apostle John sees the Ark of the Covenant in heaven.

BAPTISM

Matthew 28:19-20 . . . . . .The Great Commission—Go and make disciples of all the nations, baptizing them in the name of the Father and of the Son and of the Holy Spirit.

Mark 1:4 . . . . .John the Baptist baptizes and preaches a baptism of repentance for the forgiveness of sins.

Mark 1:9-10 . . . . .John baptizes Jesus in the Jordan River. The Holy Spirit descends upon Jesus like a dove. (see Matthew 3:13-17)

Mark 16:16 . . . . .Whoever believes (accepts Jesus Christ) and is baptized will be saved, and he who does not believe will be condemned.

Luke 3:16 . . . . .Jesus will baptize with the Holy Spirit and fire.

John 1:32-34 . . . . .John baptizes with water. Jesus will baptize with the Holy Spirit.

John 3:5 . . . . .Jesus tells Nicodemus that no one can enter heaven unless he is born of water and the Holy Spirit.

Acts 2:38 . . . . .Peter says to repent and be baptized in the name of Jesus Christ so your sins may be forgiven.

Acts 10:47-48 . . . . .Peter orders baptism for the believers who receive the Holy Spirit.

1 Corinthians 12:13 . . . . .All baptism is by one Spirit into one body. There is no discrimination.

BEATITUDES

Matthew 5:1-12 . . . . .The blessed people are the poor, meek, merciful, etc.

Luke 6:20-23 . . . . .Jesus preaches to a large crowd of His disciples regarding who the blessed are.

Revelation 14:13 . . . . . . .Blessed are the dead who die in the Lord.

Revelation 20:6 . . . . .Blessed and holy are those who have a part in the first resurrection.

BLESSINGS, GOD'S

Genesis 9:1-10 . . . . .God's promise to Noah and his family.

Genesis 9:11-16 . . . . .The rainbow is God's covenant with all living creatures of every kind on earth that never again will the waters become a flood to destroy all life.

Genesis 13:14-18 . . . . . . .God promises Abram and his offspring all the land they can see.

Genesis 17:15-19 . . . . . . .God promises Abraham a son to be called Isaac (meaning laughter) when Sarah was ninety years old and Abraham was ninety-nine years old.

Exodus 6:6-8 . . . . .God promises to bring the
Israelites out from under the
yoke of the Egyptians.

Exodus 9:1-7 . . . . .God spares the herds and flocks
of the Israelites while He kills
the Egyptian's animals.

Exodus 31:1-11 . . . . .God gives the skills to various
people to make the items God
wants for His tabernacle.

Joshua 1:1-9 . . . . .God instructs Joshua to cross
the Jordan River and promises
that every place where Joshua
sets his foot will be his.

1 Kings 17:7-16 . . . . . . .God tells Elijah to stay with a
poor widow who is short of
food. The Lord provides flour
and oil for them. The jar of flour
and the jug of oil did not run out
until the rains came.

1 Kings 19:19-21 . . . . . . .God calls Elisha to go with
Elijah.

Nehemiah 1:8-9 . . . . .God promises Israel that if they
obey him, He will gather His
people from the farthest horizon
and bring them to His chosen
dwelling place. If they disobey
Him, He will scatter them.

Psalm 34:19-20 . . . . .A righteous man may have
many troubles, but the Lord
delivers him from them all.

Isaiah 46:4 . . . . .Even in old age and gray hair, God will sustain you and rescue you.

Jeremiah 5:24 . . . . .God gives fall and spring rains and regular weeks of harvest.

Jeremiah 29:4-14 . . . . . . .God says to those He carries into exile from Jerusalem to Babylon that after seventy years of captivity, He will bring them back.

Ezekiel 1:4-28 . . . . .The Lord makes a spectacular appearance just before He calls Ezekiel to serve Him.

Ezekiel 3:1-3 . . . . .God has Ezekiel eat the scroll and it is as sweet as honey.

Ezekiel 36:26-27 . . . . . . .God gives the Israelites a new spirit with hearts of love.

Matthew 5:1-12 . . . . . . .The Beatitudes list the blessed: meek, merciful, peacemakers, etc.

Luke 1:41 . . . . .The unborn John the Baptist leaps in Elizabeth's womb when greeted by Mary. Mary is blessed among women.

Luke 12:48 . . . . .From a person who is entrusted with much, much more will be asked.

Philippians 3:20 . . . . . . .The citizenship of believers is in heaven.

James 1:12 . . . . .Blessed is the man who perseveres under trial, because when he stands the test, he will receive the crown of life.

CHURCH

Matthew 16:18 . . . . .Christ will build His church
upon the rock of Peter's faith
and confession of Jesus as the
Christ, the Son of the living
God, and the gates of Hades will
not overcome it.

Matthew 28:19 . . . . . . .Jesus commissions the church in
the Great Commission to go and
make disciples of all the nations.

Acts 8:1 . . . . .Persecution breaks out against
the church in Jerusalem and all
except the apostles are scattered
throughout Judea and Samaria.

Acts 11:25-26 . . . . .Christians are first called by that
name in Antioch.

1 Corinthians 6:1-8 . . . . .Settle disputes among yourselves within the church. Do not
take your problems before the
ungodly.

1 Corinthians 9:14 . . . . . .The Lord commands that those
who preach the gospel should
receive their living from the
gospel (see 1 Timothy 5:17-18).

Ephesians 3:6 . . . . .Through the gospel, Gentiles are
heirs together with Israelites.

1Timothy 3:1-12 . . . . . . .Guidelines for serving in
Christian leadership. A leader
must not be a recent convert (see
Titus 1:5-9).

1 Timothy 5:16 . . . . .The relatives of widows should take care of her. This is not the church's job.

Hebrews 8:5 . . . . .Our sanctuary is a copy and a shadow of what is in heaven.

Hebrews 10:24-25 . . . . . .Christians should encourage each other and meet together.

Revelation 3:15-16 . . . . .If you are spiritually lukewarm, Jesus will spit you out of His mouth.

Revelation 21:22 . . . . . . .There are no temples (churches) in heaven. God Almighty and the Lamb (Jesus) are its temple.

CIRCUMCISION

Genesis 17:9-14 . . . . .God's rule on circumcision is a covenant between Abraham and his descendants. Every male must be circumcised at eight days old. This is an everlasting covenant.

Acts 7:8 . . . . .Abraham is given the covenant of circumcision.

1 Corinthians 7:19 . . . . . .Circumcision is nothing, uncircumcision is nothing. Keeping God's commands is what counts (see Acts 15:1, 10-11).

Galatians 6:15-16 . . . . . .Circumcision is now unnecessary. What counts is a new creation in Jesus Christ.

CONFESSION

2 Samuel 12:13 . . . . .King David confesses to Nathan his sin with Bathsheba. The Lord takes away David's sin, but his son will die.

Ezra 10:11 . . . . .Confess to the Lord and do His will.

Nehemiah 9:2 . . . . .The Israelites confess their sins and the wickedness of their fathers to the Lord God.

Psalm 32:5 . . . . .Acknowledge your sin before God and confess your transgressions to the Lord, and He will forgive the guilt of your sin.

Proverbs 28:13 . . . . . . .He who conceals his sins does not prosper, but whoever confesses and renounces them finds mercy.

Matthew 10:32 . . . . . . .Acknowledge Christ before men, and He will acknowledge you before God.

Matthew 27:3-5 . . . . . . .Judas' remorse for betraying Jesus. Judas hangs himself.

Luke 18:13 . . . . .A tax collector asks God to have mercy on him, a sinner.

Romans 10:9 . . . . .If you confess with your mouth "Jesus is Lord" and believe in your heart that God raised Him from the dead, you will be saved.

2 Corinthians 9:13 . . . . . .Obedience should accompany
our confession of the gospel of
Christ.

James 5:16 . . . . .Confess your sins to each other
and pray for each other so you
may be healed.

1 John 1:9... . . . . .If we confess our sins, God is
faithful and just and will forgive
us our sins and purify us from
all unrighteousness.

CREATION

Genesis 1:1-30 . . . . .God creates the earth and everything in it.

Genesis 2:7 . . . . .God forms man from the dust of
the ground and breathes life into
him.

Genesis 2:21-22 . . . . . . .God creates woman from one of
Adam's ribs.

Genesis 3:21 . . . . .God makes the first clothes for
Adam and Eve after they sin and
realize their nakedness.

Genesis 5:1 . . . . .God creates man in the likeness
of God.

Exodus 20:11 . . . . .Creation is completed by the
Lord in six days.

Psalm 8:4-5 . . . . .God makes man a little lower
than heavenly beings.

Psalm 90:2 . . . . .God exists before creation.

Isaiah 44:24 . . . . .God alone is the creator of the heavens and the earth.

Isaiah 48:12-13 . . . . . . .God's own hand lays the foundation of the earth. His right hand spreads out the heavens.

Isaiah 65:17-25 . . . . . . .God will create new heavens and a new earth. There will be no more suffering

Jeremiah 1:5 . . . . .God tells Jeremiah that He knew him before He formed him in the womb. Before he was born, God set him apart as a prophet to the nations.

Jeremiah 5:24 . . . . .God gives fall and spring rains and regular weeks of harvest.

John 1:1-3 . . . . .Jesus is with God during creation (see Colossians 1:16).

John 8:57-58 . . . . .Jesus is in existence before Abraham was born.

Hebrews 11:3 . . . . .By faith the universe is formed at God's command, so that what is seen is not made out of what is visible.

1 Peter 1:20 . . . . .Jesus is chosen before the creation of the world, but revealed in these last times for our sake.

CRUCIFIXION

Matthew 20:19 . . . . . . .Jesus predicts that He will be turned over to the Gentiles to be mocked and flogged and cruci-

1 Corinthians 2:8 . . . . . . .None of the rulers understand or they would not have crucified the Lord of Glory (see 1 Corinthians 2:19).

Galatians 2:20 . . . . .We are crucified with Christ and no longer live, but Christ lives in us.

DEATH

Genesis 2:17 . . . . . .God warns Adam that he will surely die if he eats from the tree of knowledge of good and evil.

Genesis 3:19 . . . . .God tells Adam that he will return to the dust of the ground in death from which he was taken.

Genesis 3:19-24 . . . . .God banishes Adam and Eve from the garden. Physical death is now invoked by God upon all mankind (see verse 22).

Numbers 20:24-29 . . . . . .Because Moses and Aaron rebel against God at the waters of Meribah, God takes Aaron to Mount Hor to be gathered to his people. Aaron dies there.

Deuteronomy 17:6 . . . . . .No one will be put to death on the testimony of only one witness.

Deuteronomy 21:22-23 . .Anyone hung on a tree is under God's curse (see Galatians 3:13).

Judges 2:10 . . . . .Another term for death is "gathered to their fathers."

Psalm 116:15 . . . . .Death of the saints is precious to the Lord.

Ecclesiastes 7:1-2 . . . . . .A good name is better than perfume, and the day of death is better than the day of birth. Death is the destiny of everyone.

Isaiah 25:8 . . . . .God will end death forever.

Isaiah 57:1-2 . . . . .Devout men are taken away in death to be spared from evil.

Jeremiah 31:30 . . . . . . .Everyone shall die for his own sins.

Ezekiel 18:21 . . . . .If a wicked man turns away from all the sins he has committed and keeps all the decrees of God, he will surely live. He will not die. None of the offenses he has committed will be remembered against him.

Ezekiel 18:24 . . . . .If a righteous man turns from his righteousness and commits sin, none of the righteous things he has done will be remembered. He will die.

Matthew 10:28 . . . . . . .Do not be afraid of those who kill the body but cannot kill the soul. Rather, be afraid of God, who can destroy both the soul and body in hell.

Mark 6:21-28 . . . . King Herod has John the Baptist beheaded for a promise the king makes to his new wife's daughter.

Luke 12:4-5 . . . . Fear God, who has the power to kill your body and soul, then throw you into hell.

Luke 12:20 . . . . Fools do not plan for death.

John 8:23-24 . . . . If you do not believe in Christ, you will die in your sins.

John 14:2-3 . . . . Christ has prepared a place for believers and will take us there.

Acts 4:10 . . . . God raises Jesus from the dead after He is crucified.

Acts 5:1-11 . . . . Ananias and Sapphira both lie and withhold money from the Lord. As a result, they fall dead at Peter's feet.

Acts 7:51-53 . . . . Stephen is the first recorded martyr for Jesus.

Acts 7:54-60 . . . . Stephen is killed for standing firm for Jesus (see Acts 7:1-60).

Acts 12:21-23 . . . . An angel of the Lord strikes down King Herod. He is eaten by worms and dies.

Romans 5:12-14 . . . . . . Death is caused by Adam's sin.

Galatians 3:13 . . . . Christ redeemed us from the curse of the law by becoming a curse for us.

Philippians 2:8 . . . . Christ humbles himself in His death on the cross.

Hebrews 2:15 . . . . The fear of death is slavery.

Hebrews 9:27 . . . . Man is destined to die once, and after that to face judgment.

Hebrews 11:5 . . . . Enoch did not experience death. God took him away.

1 Peter 3:19-20 . . . . While Jesus is in the tomb He preaches to the spirits in (hell) Hades (see Ephesians 4:9).

Revelation 1:18 . . . . Jesus holds the keys to death and hell.

Revelation 2:11 . . . . The faithful Christian who overcomes will not be hurt by the second death (hell).

Revelation 20:14-15 . . . . Death and Hades will be thrown into the Lake of Fire. The Lake of Fire is the second death. Anyone whose name is not found written in the Book of Life will be thrown into the Lake of Fire.

Revelation 21:1-4 . . . . . . In heaven there will be no more death or mourning or crying or pain.

Revelation 21:8 . . . . The cowardly, the unbelieving, the vile, the murderers, the sexually immoral, those who practice magic arts, the idolaters, and all liars will be thrown into the lake of burning sulfur. This is the second death.

DECEITFULNESS

Judges 16:1 . . . . Samson falls in love with Delilah and she betrays him.

Psalm 26:4 . . . . King David says he does not sit with deceitful men nor consort with hypocrites.

Psalm 52:2-5 . . . . God will severely punish the deceitful person.

Psalm 119:29-30 . . . . Keep away from deceitful ways and set your heart on God's laws.

Proverbs 21:2 . . . . All of a man's ways seems right to him, but the Lord weighs his heart.

Proverbs 26:23 . . . . Pretty words may hide an evil heart.

Proverbs 26:28 . . . . Flattery is a form of hatred.

Isaiah 29:13 . . . . Some people honor the Lord with their mouth and lips, but their hearts are far from Him. Their worship is made up of rules taught by men (see Matthew 15:8; Mark 7:6).

Jeremiah 9:8 . . . . The deceiver speaks cordially to his neighbor but in his heart sets a trap for him.

Jeremiah 17:9-10 . . . . The heart is deceitful and beyond cure. The Lord searches the heart and examines the mind to reward a man according to his conduct.

Micah 6:10-14, 7:1-4 . . . .God's dealing with wicked Israel and man's crooked ways is applicable today.

Matthew 24:4 . . . . .Jesus says, "Watch out that no one deceives you."

Mark 4:19 . . . . .The deceitfulness of wealth and the desires of other things come in and choke God's Word.

Mark 7:22-23 . . . . .Deceit comes from inside a man and makes him unclean.

Luke 21:8 . . . . .Watch out that you are not deceived. For many will come in Jesus' name, claiming to be Him.

Romans 16:17-19 . . . . . .Smooth talk and flattery will deceive the minds of naive people. Be wise about what is good and innocent about what is evil.

2 Corinthians 11:3 . . . . .Eve is deceived by Satan's cunning.

Colossians 2:4 . . . . .Do not be deceived by fine sounding arguments.

2 Thessalonians 2:9-12 . .The antichrist will deceive with counterfeit miracles, signs and wonders. All who do not believe the truth will be condemned.

DEMONS

1 Samuel 16:14-15 . . . . . The Spirit of the Lord leaves King Saul, and an evil spirit from the Lord torments him (see 1 Samuel 18:10-11, 19:9-10).

Psalm 106:37 . . . . Parents sacrifice their children to demons (see Jeremiah 19:5).

Matthew 8:28-34 . . . . Jesus heals two violent and demon-possessed men. The demons are sent into a herd of pigs, which run off a steep bank into the lake and drown (see Mark 5:2-20; Luke 8:30-33).

Matthew 9:32-33 . . . . Jesus drives a demon out of a blind and mute man.

Matthew 10:1 . . . . Jesus gives His twelve disciples the authority to drive out evil spirits and to cure every kind of disease and sickness.

Mark 16:9 . . . . Jesus drives out seven demons from Mary Magdalene (see Luke 8:2).

Luke 4:33-36 . . . . Demons recognize Jesus as God's Holy One.

Acts 19:11-13 . . . . God uses Paul to drive out evil spirits from sick people. Handkerchiefs and aprons that touch Paul are taken to the sick and their illnesses are cured and evil spirits leave them.

2 Corinthians 11:14-15 . .Satan masquerades as an angel
of light and his servants as ser-
vants of righteousness.

1 Timothy 4:1 . . . . .In the later times some will
abandon the faith and follow
deceiving spirits and things
taught by demons.

DINOSAURS

Job 40:15-24 . . . . .The dinosaur is the "behemoth."

Job 41:1-34 . . . . .The leviathan is possibly a huge
sea mammal or dragon. Verse 21
states that flames dart from its
mouth.

DISCIPLINE

Exodus 32:25 . . . . .Aaron lets the people get out of
control. Israel thus becomes a
laughingstock to their enemies.

Leviticus 24:14-16 . . . . . .Anyone who curses the name of
the Lord must be put to death.

Deuteronomy 4:36 . . . . . .God makes you hear His voice
to discipline you.

Judges 8:16 . . . . .Gideon punishes the men of
Succoth with desert thorns and
briers.

Ezra 7:26 . . . . .Whoever does not obey the law
of God and the law of the king
will be punished by death, ban-
ishment, confiscation of property, or imprisonment.

Psalm 89:32-33 . . . . .God will punish our sins with the rod and flogging, but He will not take His love away.

Psalm 94:12 . . . . .Blessed is the man God disciplines

Proverbs 1:7 . . . . .The fear of the Lord is the beginning of knowledge, but fools despise wisdom and discipline.

Proverbs 3:11 . . . . .Do not despise the Lord's discipline, and do not resent His rebuke.

Proverb 3:12 . . . . .The Lord disciplines those He loves.

Proverbs 10:17 . . . . . . .He who heeds discipline shows the way to life, but whoever ignores correction leads others astray.

Proverbs 12:1 . . . . .Whoever loves discipline loves knowledge, but he who hates correction is stupid (see Proverbs 15:32).

Proverbs 13:1 . . . . .A wise son heeds his father's instruction, but a mocker does not listen to rebuke.

Proverbs 13:24 . . . . . . .He who spares the rod hates his son, but he who loves him is careful to discipline him.

Proverbs 22:15 . . . . . . .Folly is bound up in the heart of a child, but the rod of discipline will drive it from him.

Proverbs 23:13-14 . . . . . .Do not withhold punishment from a child. If you punish him with a rod, he will not die. Punish him with the rod and save his soul from death.

Proverbs 26:3 . . . . .A whip for the horse, a bridle for the donkey, and a rod for the backs of fools.

Proverbs 29:15 . . . . .The rod of correction imparts wisdom, but children left to themselves disgrace their mothers.

Proverbs 29:17 . . . . .Discipline your son and he will give you peace. He will bring delight to your soul.

Jeremiah 30:11 . . . . .God disciplines with justice.

Galatians 5:15 . . . . .Christians fighting each other will destroy each other.

Colossians 3:2-4 . . . . . .Set your mind on heaven, not on things of this world.

Colossians 3:5 . . . . .Put to death whatever belongs to your earthly nature: sexual immorality, impurity, lust, evil desires and greed.

Colossians 4:6 . . . . .Let your conversation be always full of grace and seasoned with salt

1 Thessalonians 4:11-12 .Lead a quiet life. Mind your own business.

1 Timothy 1:3-4 . . . . .Do not teach false doctrines or be devoted to myths and endless genealogies.

Hebrews 12:5-13 . . . . . . .The lord disciplines everyone He accepts as a son.

Revelation 3:19 . . . . .God rebukes and disciplines those He loves.

DIVORCE

Deuteronomy 24:1-4 . . . .A man and wife once divorced from each other are not allowed to remarry each other if they have remarried and divorced again (see Jeremiah 3:1).

Malachi 2:16 . . . . .The Lord God hates divorce.

Matthew 5:31 . . . . .Anyone who divorces his wife must give her a certificate of divorce.

Matthew 5:32 . . . . .Anyone who divorces his wife, except for marital unfaithfulness, causes her to commit adultery. Anyone who marries a woman so divorced commits adultery (see Matthew 19:9).

Romans 7:1-2 . . . . .A married woman is bound to her husband as long as he is alive, but if her husband dies, she is released from the law of marriage.

EATING FOOD/MEAT

2 Samuel 6:19 . . . . .King David gives food to a
crowd of Israelites, including a
cake of raisins to everyone.

2 Samuel 16:1 . . . . .King David receives supplies,
including a hundred cakes of
raisins.

Jeremiah 49:9 . . . . .Grape pickers will leave a few
grapes (see Obadiah 5).

Daniel 1:8-16 . . . . .Daniel, Shadrach, Meshach, and
Abednego eat only vegetables,
no meat, while in Babylon.

Hosea 3:1 . . . . .In some circles raisin cakes are
considered sacred.

Mark 7:17-23 . . . . .Nothing taken from outside the
body is unclean. In saying this,
Jesus declares all foods clean.
What comes out of a man is
what makes him unclean. For
from within, out of men's hearts,
come evil thoughts (sexual
immorality, greed, envy, etc.).

Acts 10:9-16 . . . . .Peter's vision. Do not call anything impure that God has made
clean.

Romans 14:15 . . . . .Do not offend your brother by
what you eat.

Romans 14:19-21 . . . . . .It is wrong for a man to eat anything that causes someone else
to stumble.

1 Corinthians 8:4-9 . . . . .It is all right to eat meat that has
been sacrificed to idols, since

they are false gods. Be careful
not to exercise your freedom to
eat anything if it becomes a
stumbling block to the weak
(see 1 Corinthians 10:25-26).

1 Corinthians 8:10-13 . . .Do not offend your brother by
what you eat.

1 Timothy 4:3-5 . . . . .Everything that God created is
good.

ENEMIES

Joshua 6:2-20 . . . . .God says to Joshua that the
Israelites are to march around
the city of Jericho once each day
for six days. On the seventh day
they are to march around the
city walls seven times, then give
a loud shout, and the walls of
the city will collapse.

Joshua 6:21-26 . . . . .The Israelites kill every   living
thing in Jericho—men, women,
young and old, livestock—
except Rahab the prostitute and
her family.

Joshua 8:24-25 . . . . .The Israelites kill all men and
women, everyone who lives in Ai.

Joshua 10:10-11 . . . . . . .The Lord throws Israel's enemies into confusion by throwing
large hailstones from heaven to
kill them.

Joshua 10:12-13 . . . . . . .The Lord makes the sun and
moon stand still until Israel
avenges itself against its
enemies.

Judges 15:4 . . . . .Samson catches three hundred
foxes and ties them tail to tail in
pairs, fastens a torch to every
pair, lights the torches and turns
them loose in the standing grain
of the Philistines.

Judges 15:13-16 . . . . . . .Samson kills one thousand
Philistines with the jawbone of a
donkey.

Judges 16:4-21 . . . . .The Philistines gouge out
Samson's eyes.

Psalm 23:1-6 . . . . .The Lord comforts us as He
deals with our enemies.

Proverbs 16:7 . . . . .When a man's ways are pleasing to the Lord, He makes even
his enemies live at peace with
him.

Proverbs 24:1-22 . . . . . . .The Lord will deal with our
enemies.

Matthew 5:44 . . . . .Love your enemies (see Luke
6:27).

Matthew 10:28 . . . . . . .Do not be afraid of enemies who
kill the body, not the soul.
Rather, be afraid of the God,
who can destroy both the soul
and body in hell.

EXODUS

people go with them. The
Israelites live in Egypt for 430
years.

Exodus 13:18-22 . . . .God leads his people out of
Egypt. He goes ahead in a pillar
of a cloud by day and a pillar of
fire by night. The pillar is always
in front of the Israelites.

Exodus 14:10-31 . . . . . . .God has Moses part the Red Sea,
and God kills the Egyptian army.

Exodus 14:19 . . . . .The pillar of cloud moves from in
front and stands behind the
Israelites, coming between the
armies of Egypt and Israel.

Exodus 14:20 . . . . . . .Throughout the night the cloud
brings darkness to the one side
(Egyptians) and light to the other
side (Israelites).

Exodus 14:25 . . . . .God makes the chariot wheels of
the Egyptians swerve so they
have difficulty driving.

FAITH

Jeremiah 17:7 . . . . .Blessed is the man who trusts in
the Lord.

Psalm 118:8 . . . . .Take refuge in the Lord rather
than trust in man.

Matthew 15:21-28 . . . . . .Jesus acknowledges the faith of
a Canaanite woman.

when the Egyptians try it, they
perish.

Hebrews 11:30 . . . . .By faith, the walls of Jericho fell
after the people marched around
it for seven days.

2 Peter 1:3-11 . . . . .Add to your faith goodness. To
goodness add knowledge. To
knowledge add self-control. To
self-control add perseverance.
To perseverance add godliness.
To godliness add brotherly kindness. To brotherly kindness add
love.

FEAR

Psalm 34:11-14 . . . . . . .Fear the Lord. Keep your tongue
from evil and your lips from
speaking lies. Turn from evil
and do good.

Psalm 55:4-8 . . . . .King David expresses his fear
and how it affects him.

Psalm 147:11 . . . . .The Lord delights in those who
fear him, who put their hope in
his unfailing love.

Proverbs 1:7 . . . . .The fear of the Lord is the
beginning of knowledge, but
fools despise wisdom and discipline.

Proverbs 3:7 . . . . .Do not be wise in your own
eyes. Fear the Lord and shun
evil.

Proverbs 3:25 . . . . .Have no fear of sudden
disasters.

Proverbs 15:33 . . . . .The fear of the Lord teaches
man wisdom, and humility
comes before honor.

Matthew 6:34 . . . . .Do not worry about tomorrow,
for tomorrow will worry about
itself. Each day has enough trouble of its own.

Luke 12:4-5 . . . . .Do not fear those who kill the
body and after that can do no
more. Rather, fear God, who,
after killing the body, has power
to throw you into hell.

Hebrews 2:15 . . . . .The fear of death is slavery.

1 John 4:18 . . . . .There is no fear in love. But perfect love drives out fear, because
fear has to do with punishment.
The man who fears is not made
perfect in love.

Revelation 14:7 . . . . .Fear God and give him glory,
because the hour of his judg-
ment has come. Worship him
who made the heavens, the
earth, the sea, and the springs of
water.

FLOOD, GREAT

Genesis 6:13-16 . . . . .God tells Noah He is going to
destroy the earth. He instructs
Noah to build an Ark of cypress

wood. The Ark is to be 450 feet long, seventy-five feet wide, and forty-five feet high.

Genesis 6:17-22 . . . . .God informs Noah that He is going to bring floodwaters on the earth to destroy all life under the heavens. His wife and sons and their wives will be on the Ark with Noah.

Genesis 6:19-22 . . . . .Noah is to bring into the Ark two animals of every kind, both male and female.

Genesis 7:1-4 . . . . .God instructs Noah to take seven pairs of every kind of clean animal and two of every kind of unclean animal in the Ark (see Leviticus 11:4-41).

Genesis 7:8-10 . . . . .The animals go into the Ark with Noah.

Genesis 7:12 . . . . .Rain falls on the earth forty days and forty nights.

Genesis 7:20 . . . . .Floodwaters cover the mountains to a depth of more than twenty feet.

Genesis 7:24 . . . . .The waters flood the earth for 150 days.

Genesis 8:4 . . . . .The Ark comes to rest on the mountains of Ararat on the seventeenth day of the seventh month.

Genesis 8:5 . . . . The floodwaters recede below the tops of the mountains on the first day of the tenth month.

Genesis 8:13 . . . . By the first day of the first month of Noah's six hundred and first year, the waters dry up from the earth.

Genesis 8:14 . . . . The earth is completely dry by the twenty-seventh day of the second month of Noah's six hundred and first year.

Genesis 9:2-3 . . . . All animals including birds and fish will fear Noah (man). Everything that lives will be food for you.

Genesis 9:11 . . . . God promises never again to flood the entire earth.

Genesis 9:13-16 . . . . God promises to set a rainbow in the clouds as a covenant between Him and the earth that never again will the waters become a flood to destroy all life.

Isaiah 54:9 . . . . God swears that the floodwaters would never again cover the earth.

FOOLS

Leviticus 19:28 . . . . Do not put tattoo marks on yourself.

Psalm 53:1 . . . . .The fool says in his heart, "There is no God."

Proverbs 10:14 . . . . .Wise men store up knowledge, but the mouth of a fool invites trouble.

Proverbs 10:23 . . . . .A fool finds pleasure in evil conduct.

Proverbs 12:15 . . . . .The way of a fool seems right to him, but a wise man listens to advice.

Proverbs 12:23 . . . . .A prudent man keeps his knowledge to himself, but the hearts of fools blurt out folly.

Proverbs 21:20 . . . . .A foolish man devours all he has.

Proverbs 23:9 . . . . .Do not speak to a fool, for he will scorn the wisdom of your words.

Proverbs 27:12 . . . . .Prudent people see danger and take refuge. Simple people keep going and suffer for it.

Ecclesiastes 10:2 . . . . . . .The heart of the wise inclines him to the right, but the heart of the fool to the left.

Isaiah 32:6 . . . . .Fools speak folly, their minds are busy with evil, and they practice ungodliness.

Jeremiah 17:11 . . . . .A man's riches gained by unjust means will be lost when his life is half gone. In the end, he will prove to be a fool.

Luke 12:13-21 . . . . .The story of the rich fool who stores up things for himself but is not rich toward God.

Luke 12:20 . . . . .Fools do not plan for death.

Romans 1:21-22 . . . . . . .Although they know God, they neither glorify him nor give thanks to him. They claim to be wise but become fools.

Romans 11:7-8 . . . . .God gives a spirit of stupor to unbelievers.

1 Corinthians 1:27 . . . . . .God chooses the foolish things of the world to shame the wise, and the weak things of the world to shame the strong.

FORGIVENESS

2 Chronicles 7:14 . . . . . .If God's people call on his name, humble themselves, pray, seek his face, and turn from their wicked ways, then will God hear them and will forgive their sins and will heal their land.

Jeremiah 5:1 . . . . .God will forgive Jerusalem if one honest person exists.

Matthew 6:12 . . . . .Forgive us our debts, as we forgive our debtors.

Matthew 6:14-15 . . . . . . .If we forgive those who sin against us, God will also forgive us. If we do not forgive men

their sins, God will
not forgive our sins.

Matthew 18:21-22 . . . . . .Peter asks Jesus, "How many
times shall I forgive my brother
when he sins against me?" Jesus
answers, "Forgive seventy-seven
times."

Mark 3:28-29 . . . . .All the sins and blasphemes of
men will be forgiven them, but
whoever blasphemes the Holy
Spirit will never be forgiven. He
is guilty of an eternal sin.

Mark 11:25 . . . . .When we stand praying, if we
hold anything against anyone,
forgive him, so that God may
forgive your sins.

Luke 11:4 . . . . .Forgive us our sins, for we also
forgive everyone who sins
against us. And lead us not into
temptation.

Luke 23:34 . . . . .Jesus says, "Father, forgive
them, for they do not know what
they are doing."

Romans 12:17-19 . . . . . .Do not repay anyone evil for
evil. Do not take revenge. Leave
room for God's wrath (see 1
Peter 3:9).

Ephesians 1:7 . . . . .We have redemption through
Jesus' blood, the forgiveness of
sins, in accordance with the
riches of God's grace.

Colossians 3:13 . . . . .Forgive each other whatever
grievances you may have against
one another. Forgive as the Lord
forgave you.

1 John 1:7 . . . . .If believers walk in the light
with Christ Jesus, He will purify
us from every sin.

1 John 1:9 . . . . .If believers confess their sins,
God is faithful and just and will
forgive their sins and purify
them from all unrighteousness.

GIVING/TITHES

Genesis 14:20 . . . . .Abraham gives a tenth of everything.

Genesis 28:20-22 . . . . . .Jacob vows to give a tenth of
everything upon his safe return.

Leviticus 27:30-34 . . . . . .The Lord gives a command to
Moses regarding tithing. A tenth
of everything from the land
belongs to the Lord. It is Holy to
the Lord.

Numbers 18:25-29 . . . . . .The Lord tells Moses to instruct
the Levites that when they
receive a tithe from the
Israelites, they must present the
best tenth of that tithe to the
Lord.

2 Chronicles 31:5 . . . . . .King Hezekiah orders the
Israelites to tithe, and they
respond generously.

Nehemiah 10:38-39 . . . . .The Levites are instructed to receive the Israelite's tithes.

Proverbs 3:9-10 . . . . .Honor the Lord with your wealth and your first fruits. Then your barns will be filled to overflowing.

Malachi 3:9-12 . . . . .Do not rob the Lord. Bring the whole tithe to the Lord, and He will bless you.

Matthew 6:1-4 . . . . .Give to the needy quietly, and God who sees you will reward you.

Matthew 10:9-10 . . . . . . .Those who are helped by the disciples should take care of the needs of the disciples. The worker is worth his keep.

Matthew 23:23 . . . . .Woe to the teachers of the law and Pharisees who give a tenth but neglect justice, mercy, and faithfulness.

Luke 11:42 . . . . .Woe to the Pharisees, because you give a tenth, but you neglect justice and the love of God.

Luke 12:34 . . . . .Where your treasures is, there your heart will be also.

Luke 21:2-4 . . . . .The poor widow's gift of two copper coins is more than all the rest in the Lord's eyes because she trusts Him with all she has.

1 Corinthians 9:14 . . . . . .Those who preach the gospel should receive their living from the gospel.

1 Corinthians 16:1-4 . . . .Paul instructs the churches about saving up for their giving.

2 Corinthians 8:1-12 . . . .Paul tells about the generosity of the Macedonian churches.

2 Corinthians 9:6-8 . . . . .Whoever sows sparingly will reap sparingly, and whoever sows generously will reap generously. God loves a cheerful giver.

Hebrews 7:5-6 . . . . .The priests who are the descendants of Levi are to collect a tenth from the people.

GOD

Genesis 1:1-31 . . . . .God creates all things.

Exodus 3:13-15 . . . . .God tells Moses that He is the "I AM." He is the God of Abraham, the God of Isaac, and the God of Jacob.

Exodus 6:3 . . . . .Two of God's names are "God Almighty" and "Lord."

Job 22:21 . . . . .Submit to God and be at peace with Him. In this way prosperity will come to you.

Psalm 30:5 . . . . .God's anger lasts only a moment, but His favor lasts a lifetime.

Psalm 47:2 . . . . .How awesome is the Lord Most
High, the great King over all the
earth!

Psalm 54:4 . . . . .Surely God is my help. The
Lord is the one who sustains me.

Ecclesiastes 3:11 . . . . . . .God has set eternity in the hearts
of men. Yet they cannot fathom
what God has done from beginning to end.

Isaiah 46:5 . . . . .God is incomparable. To whom
will you compare God or count
Him equal?

Isaiah 55:8-9 . . . . .As the heavens are higher than
the earth, God's thoughts and
ways are above our thoughts and
ways.

Isaiah 64:4 . . . . .No one has heard, no ear has
perceived, no eye has seen any
God besides you.

Amos 4:13 . . . . .God forms the mountains, creates the wind, reveals His
thoughts to man, turns dawn to
darkness. The Lord God
Almighty is His name.

Matthew 5:45 . . . . .God causes the sun to rise on
the evil and good and sends rain
on the righteous and unrighteous.

John 10:30 . . . . .Jesus says that He and the
Father are one.

John 14:9-12 . . . . .Jesus is in the Father and the Father is in Jesus. Anyone who has seen Jesus has seen the Father.

Romans 11:22 . . . . .Consider the kindness and sternness of God. Sternness to those who fell, but kindness to you (believers), provided that you continue in His kindness.

1 Timothy 2:5 . . . . .There is one God and one mediator between God and men, the man Christ Jesus.

1 John 3:1-3 . . . . .We are children of God. The reason the world does not know us is that it did not know Him.

GOVERNMENTS, WORLDLY

1 Samuel 8:4-22 . . . . . . .The Hebrews want an earthly king like the pagans. God tells Samuel to give them one. This was the beginning of godly nations being ruled by appointed or elected men rather than God himself or His appointed prophets or judges.

1 Samuel 10:1 . . . . .Samuel anoints Saul (not the same Saul/Paul of the New Testament) as the first King of Israel (1 Samuel 11:14-15).

1 Samuel 12:17 . . . . . . .Samuel tells the Hebrews what an evil thing they did by wanting an earthly king.

Acts 5:29 . . . . .We must obey God over men
(governments).

Romans 13:1-2 . . . . .Submit to governing authorities.
God creates all authorities.

GRACE

Nehemiah 9:17 . . . . .God is gracious and compas-
sionate, slow to anger and
abounding in love.

Psalm 145:8-9 . . . . .The Lord is gracious and com-
passionate, slow to anger and
rich in love.

John 1:16 . . . . .From the fullness of the Lord's
grace we all receive one blessing
after another.

Acts 15:10-11 . . . . .We are saved through the grace
of our Lord Jesus.

Romans 1:5 . . . . .Through Christ we receive grace
and apostleship to call people
from among all the Gentiles to
the obedience that comes from
faith.

Romans 5:17 . . . . .God's abundant grace and the
gift of righteousness reign in life
through Jesus Christ.

2 Corinthians 6:1 . . . . . . .Do not receive God's grace in
vain. If we claim to believe the
gospel but never demonstrate its
affects in our lives, what good
has it done?

Ephesians 1:7-8 . . . . .In Christ we have redemption through His blood, the forgiveness of sins, in accordance with His grace.

Ephesians 2:8-9 . . . . .For it is by grace you have been saved through faith, not from yourselves. It is the gift of God, not by works so no one can boast.

GREED

Psalm 52:7 . . . . .Do not trust in your own wealth and grow strong by destroying others.

Psalm 119:36 . . . . .Turn your heart toward God's statutes and not toward selfish gain.

Proverbs 15:27 . . . . .A greedy man brings trouble to his family, but he who hates bribes will live.

Proverbs 23:4 . . . . .Do not wear yourself out to get rich. Have wisdom and show restraint.

Proverbs 28:19 . . . . .A person who chases fantasies will have his fill of poverty.

Proverbs 28:20 . . . . .A greedy person tries to get rich quick.

Ecclesiastes 5:10 . . . . . . .Whoever loves money never has enough. Whoever loves wealth is never satisfied with his income.

Ezekiel 34:2 . . . . .The Lord says, "Woe to the shepherds (spiritual and political leaders) of Israel who only take care of themselves! Should not shepherds take care of the flock (people)?"

Matthew 6:19-20 . . . . . . .Do not store up for yourselves treasures on earth, but store up for yourselves treasures in heaven.

Matthew 6:21 . . . . .For where your treasure is, there your heart will be also.

Matthew 6:24 . . . . .You cannot serve both God and money.

Luke 12:13-20 . . . . .Jesus says, "Watch out! Be on your guard against all kinds of greed. A man's life does not consist in the abundance of his possessions."

Luke 12:21 . . . . .Store up riches toward God, not for yourself.

Colossians 3:5 . . . . .Put to death whatever belongs to your earthly nature: sexual immorality, impurity, lust, evil desires and greed, which is idolatry.

1 Timothy 6:9 . . . . .People who want to get rich fall into temptation and a trap and into many foolish and harmful desires that plunge men into ruin and destruction.

1 Timothy 6:10 . . . . .For the love of money is a root
of all kinds of evil.

Hebrews 13:5 . . . . .Keep your lives free from the
love of money and be content
with what you have.

James 4:1-2 . . . . .Fights and quarrels come from
our own desires within us. We
do not have, because we do not
ask God. We ask with wrong
motives.

HEAVEN

Genesis 1:1 . . . . .In the beginning, God creates
the heavens and the earth.

Genesis 7:11 . . . . .The floodgates of heaven open
up and all the springs of the
great deep burst forth and rain
falls on the earth forty days and
forty nights in the six hundredth
year of Noah's life.

Psalm 103:11-12 . . . . . . .God will remove our transgres-
sion (sins) from us (believers),
as far as the east is from the
west.

Isaiah 43:25 . . . . .God will blot out (after repentance) our transgressions   (sins)
and remember them no more.

Matthew 10:33 . . . . .Whoever disowns Jesus before
men shall be disowned before
God in heaven.

Mark 16:19 . . . . After the Lord Jesus speaks to the disciples, He is taken up into heaven and He sits at the right hand of God.

John 14:1-3 . . . . In God's house (heaven) there are many rooms. Jesus prepares a place for us (believers), so we will be with Him in heaven.

1 Corinthians 2:9 . . . . No eye has seen, no ear has heard, no mind conceives what God has prepared for those who love Him.

1 Corinthians 6:9-11 . . . . Neither the sexually immoral nor idolaters nor adulterers nor male prostitutes nor homosexual offenders will inherit the kingdom of God (see Galatians 5:19-21; Revelation 21:8).

2 Corinthians 5:6-8 . . . . . As long as we are at home in the body we are away from the Lord. We prefer to be away from the body and at home (in heaven) with the Lord.

2 Corinthians 12:2-4 . . . . The apostle Paul is taken up to the third heaven (paradise). He hears inexpressible things that man is not permitted to tell.

Philippians 1:22-23 . . . . . The apostle Paul prefers to depart his body and be with Christ, which is better by far.

Philippians 3:20-22 . . . . .Our citizenship is in heaven. We
eagerly await a Savior from
there, the Lord Jesus Christ. He
will transform our lowly bodies
so they will be like Jesus' glorious body.

2 Peter 3:10-13 . . . . .Everything will be destroyed on
the day of the Lord and a new
heaven and new earth will be
created.

Revelation 1:1-2 . . . . . . .God gives to His servant John,
by sending His angel, the revela-
tion of Jesus Christ to show
God's servants (believers) what
soon will take place. God
reveals to the apostle John the
wonders of heaven.

Revelation 1:10 . . . . .John is in the spirit (out of the
body).

Revelation 3:11-13 . . . . .The new Jerusalem will be coming down from heaven.

Revelation 4:1-8 . . . . . . .A description of heaven by John
who is in the spirit   (out of
the body) and allowed to see
some of heaven.

Revelation 7:9 . . . . .Saved people from every nation
(all races) will be in heaven.

Revelation 12:7-9 . . . . . .Satan and his fallen angels are
thrown out of heaven down to
earth.

Revelation 21:8 . . . . The cowardly, the unbelievers, the vile, the murderers, the sexually immoral, those who practice magic arts, the idolaters, and all liars will be in the fiery lake of burning sulfur (hell).

Revelation 21:15-17 . . . . Description of the new Jerusalem. It will be about 1,400 miles long and as wide and high as it is long. The city walls will be about 200 feet thick or high.

Revelation 21:18-21 . . . . The wall is made of jasper and the city of pure gold, as pure as glass.

Revelation 21:23 . . . . The New Jerusalem (heaven) does not need the sun or the moon to shine on it, for the glory of God gives it light.

Revelation 22:1 . . . . The river of the water of life, as clear as crystal, flowing from God's throne.

Revelation 22:2 . . . . The river is flowing down the middle of the great street of the city (heaven). On each side of the river stands the Tree of Life bearing twelve crops of fruit every month.

Revelation 22:3-5 . . . . . . There will be no more night in heaven. A lamp of light from the sun will not be needed, for the Lord God will give light.

HEBREWS/ISRAELITES

Exodus 2:11-12 . . . . .Moses kills an Egyptian who is beating another Hebrew.

Exodus 33:3 . . . . .God calls the Hebrews a "stiff-necked" people.

Deuteronomy 28:63-64 . .For disobedience to God, He will scatter the Israelites among all the nations.

Deuteronomy 31:27 . . . . .Moses repeats how stiff- necked the Hebrews are.

Joshua 5:12 . . . . .God stops the manna from heaven when the Israelites eat the produce of the land of Canaan.

Judges 20:16 . . . . .Seven hundred soldiers who were left-handed could sling a stone at a hair and not miss.

1 Samuel 15:32-33 . . . . .Samuel kills King Agag of the Amalekites.

1 Samuel 15:35 . . . . .The Lord is grieved that He has made Saul king over Israel (Israel's first king).

1 Samuel 17:8-16 . . . . . .Goliath, the Philistine giant, challenges the Hebrews for forty days.

2 Kings 15:16-18 . . . . . . .King Menahem of Israel does evil in the eyes of the Lord. He attacks Tiphsah, and because they refuse to open the city gates, he sacks Tiphsah and rips open all the pregnant women.

2 Chronicles 30:7-8 . . . . .King Hezekiah tells the
Israelites not to be stiff-necked
like their fathers were, but to
submit to the Lord.

Psalm 105:12-45 . . . . . . .A recap of the Hebrews in Egypt
and God's fury and blessings.

Isaiah 22:13 . . . . .The Hebrews have a cavalier
attitude—eat and drink, for
tomorrow we die.

Ezekiel 2:1-10 . . . . .The Lord calls Ezekiel.

Acts 23:7-8 . . . . .The difference between the
Pharisees and the Sadducees is
that the Sadducees do not
believe in any type of resurrection, angels, or spirits. The
Pharisees acknowledge them all.

HELL

Matthew 7:13-14 . . . . . . .Small is the gate and narrow is
the road that leads to life. wide
is the gate and broad is the road
that leads to destruction (hell).

Matthew 10:33 . . . . .Whoever disowns Jesus before
men shall be disowned before
God in heaven.

Matthew 13:42, 50 . . . . . .Unbelievers will be thrown into
the fiery furnace, where there
will be weeping and gnashing of
teeth.

Matthew 25:41 . . . . .The wicked (non-believers) who
are cursed will be cast into the

eternal fire prepared for the devil and his angels.

Matthew 25:46 . . . . .Unbelievers will go away to eternal punishment, but the righteous to eternal life in heaven.

Luke 12:20 . . . . .Fools do not plan for death.

Luke 13:28 . . . . .There will be weeping and gnashing of teeth by those who are thrown into hell.

Luke 16:19-31 . . . . .Hell is a place of turmoil. Jesus tells His disciples the story about a beggar named Lazarus (not the same Lazarus that He raised from the dead) and a rich man. The rich man dies and went to hell where he is in torment in a fire.

John 8:23-24 . . . . .If you do not believe in Christ, you will indeed die in your sins.

1 Corinthians 6:9-11 . . . .Neither the sexually immoral nor idolaters nor adulterers nor male prostitutes nor homosexual offenders will inherit the kingdom of God (see Galatians 5:19-21; Revelation 21:8).

Ephesians 4:9 . . . . .Christ descends to the lower earthly regions (hell).

2 Thessalonians 1:8-9 . . .God will punish with everlasting destruction those who do not know Him and do not obey the gospel of our Lord Jesus.

1 Peter 3:19-20 . . . . .While Jesus is in the tomb, He preaches to the spirits in prison (hell) (see Ephesians 4:9).

2 Peter 2:4 . . . . .Hell is a place of gloomy dungeons.

Revelation 1:18 . . . . .Jesus holds the keys to death and Hades (hell).

Revelation 20:10 . . . . . . .Satan will be thrown into the Lake of Fire of burning sulfur (hell) where he and the false prophet will be tormented day and night forever.

Revelation 20:14-15 . . . .Death and Hades will be thrown into the Lake of Fire. The Lake of Fire is the second death. Anyone whose name is not found written in the Book of Life will be thrown into the Lake of Fire.

Revelation 21:8 . . . . .The cowardly, the unbelieving, the vile, the murderers, the sexually immoral, those who practice magical arts, the idolaters, and all liars will be thrown into the lake of burning sulfur.

HOLY SPIRIT

Genesis 1:2 . . . . .The Holy Spirit is with God during creation.

Judges 6:34 . . . . .The Spirit of the Lord comes upon Gideon, who blows his trumpet to summon the Abiezrites to follow him.

1 Samuel 16:14 . . . . .The Spirit of the Lord departs
from King Saul, and an evil
spirit from the Lord torments
him.

Job 32:8 . . . . .It is the spirit in a man, the
breath of the Almighty that gives
him understanding.

Ezekiel 36:27 . . . . .God will put His Spirit in us and
move us to follow His decrees
and to be careful to keep His
laws.

Matthew 1:18 . . . . .Mary, mother of Jesus Christ,
becomes pregnant through the
Holy Spirit (see Luke 1:34-35).

Matthew 3:11 . . . . .John the Baptist baptizes with
water for repentance. Jesus bap-
tizes with the Holy Spirit and
fire.

Matthew 3:16 . . . . .As soon as Jesus is baptized, He
sees the Spirit of God (Holy
Spirit) descending like a dove
and lighting on him.

Matthew 12:32 . . . . .Anyone who speaks (blasphemes) against the Holy Spirit
will not be forgiven.

Luke 4:1-2 . . . . .Jesus is full of the Holy Spirit
and is tempted by the devil for
forty days.

John 14:26 . . . . .The Counselor, the Holy Spirit,
whom God will send in the
name of Jesus, will teach all

things and remind the apostles of everything Jesus said to them.

John 16:13 . . . . When the Holy Spirit of Truth comes, He will guide the apostles into all truth. He will tell them what is yet to come.

Acts 2:1-2 . . . . The Apostles receive the Holy Spirit on the Day of Pentecost.

Acts 2:3-4 . . . . When the Holy Spirit comes on the apostles, they see what seems to be tongues of fire that separate and come to rest on each of them on the Day of Pentecost.

Acts 8:36-40 . . . . The Holy Spirit takes Philip from one place to another.

Acts 19:2-6 . . . . The apostle Paul places his hands on some disciples. They receive the Holy Spirit, speak in tongues, and prophesied.

Romans 8:26-27 . . . . The Holy Spirit guides us in prayer.

1 Corinthians 2:10-14 . . . The man without the Spirit does not accept the things that come from the Spirit of God, for they are foolish to him.

1 Corinthians 6:19-20 . . . Your body is a temple of the Holy Spirit who is in you, whom you have received from God. Therefore honor God with your body.

1 Corinthians 12:3 . . . . . .No one can say, "Jesus is Lord" except by the Holy Spirit.

Galatians 5:22-23 . . . . . .The fruit of the Spirit is love, joy, peace, patience, kindness, goodness, faithfulness, gentleness, and self-control. Against such things there is no law.

Hebrews 1:14 . . . . .All angels are ministering spirits for those who will inherit salvation.

Hebrews 10:14-17 . . . . . .The Holy Spirit testifies that God will not remember our sin.

Hebrews 13:2 . . . . .Entertain strangers. Some are angels.

HOMOSEXUALITY

Genesis 19:1-26 . . . . . . .Homosexuality is the reason Sodom and Gomorrah is destroyed (verse 5,13).

Leviticus 18:22-23 . . . . .Man must not lie with another man as one lies with a woman. That is detestable. Do not have sexual relations with an animal and defile yourself.

Leviticus 20:13 . . . . . . .If a man lies with a man as with a woman, that is detestable. They must be put to death. Their blood will be on their own heads.

Romans 1:24-27 . . . . . .Men and women exchange natural relations for unnatural ones.

Men commit indecent acts with other men and receive due penalties for their perversions.

1 Corinthians 6:9-11 . . . .The sexually immoral, idolaters, adulterers, male prostitutes, and homosexual offenders will not inherit the kingdom of God (see Galatians 5:19-21; Revelation 21:8).

Jude 7 . . . . .Sodom and Gomorrah and the surrounding towns give themselves up to sexual immorality and perversion. They serve as an example of those who suffer the punishment of eternal fire.

Revelation 21:8 . . . . .The cowardly, the unbelievers, the vile, the murderers, the sexually immoral, those who practice magical arts, the idolaters and all liars will be in the lake of burning sulfur (hell). This is the second death.

HOROSCOPES

Leviticus 19:26 . . . . .Do not practice divination or sorcery (fortune telling).

Deuteronomy 18:10 . . . . .Do not sacrifice children in the fire, practice divination or sorcery, interpret omens, or engage in witchcraft.

Deuteronomy 18:11 . . . . .Do not cast spells or associate with anyone who is a medium or

spiritist or who consults the
dead.

2 Kings 17:16-20 . . . . . . .The Hebrews fall away and
practice divination and sorcery.

Isaiah 8:19 . . . . .God says instead of consulting
mediums and spiritists, people
should inquire of God. Why
consult the dead on behalf of the
living?

Isaiah 47:13-15 . . . . .Astrologers (stargazers) cannot
save you or themselves.

Jeremiah 10:2-5 . . . . .Do not learn the ways of the
nations (worldly) or be terrified
by the signs in the sky (astrolo-
gy, horoscopes, etc.), for the
customs of the people are worthless.

Micah 5:12 . . . . .God will destroy man's witchcraft, and they will no longer
cast spells.

IDOLS

Genesis 35:2-4 . . . . .Jacob's household and all with
him give up all their foreign
gods and the rings in their ears.

Exodus 22:18 . . . . .Do not allow a sorceress to live.

Exodus 22:20 . . . . .Whoever sacrifices to any god
other than the Lord must be
destroyed.

Exodus 32:1-14 . . . . .Aaron makes a golden calf (pat-
terned after Apis, the Egyptian

bull god). God threatens to kill the people, but Moses asks for forgiveness for the people.

Exodus 32:20 . . . . .The golden calf is ground up into powder, scattered on the water, and Moses makes the Israelites drink it.

Exodus 32:30-35 . . . . . . .God will punish those who sin against Him. The Lord strikes the Israelites with a plague because they worship the golden calf that Aaron made.

Deuteronomy 7:2-4 . . . . .God orders the Israelites to destroy the Canaanite nations totally, to show them no mercy, and to refrain from intermarrying with them, for they will turn them away from following God to serve other gods.

Deuteronomy 7:5 . . . . . . .God instructs the Israelites to break down their heathen altars, smash their sacred stones, cut down their Asherah poles, and burn their idols in the fire.

Deuteronomy 8:19 . . . . . .God tells the Israelites that if they ever forget the Lord and follow other gods, the Lord will destroy them.

Deuteronomy 13:1-5 . . . .Do not follow false prophets. God will test you to see if you are loyal. Put false prophets to death.

save are ignorant. God alone is
God, and there is none other.

Isaiah 46:8-10 . . . . .God is the only God, and there
is none other. He will do all that
He pleases.

Isaiah 57:8 . . . . .God says to the Israelites that
they put their pagan gods behind
doorposts and go to bed with
pagan symbols.

Jeremiah 2:5-37 . . . . .The Hebrews follow worthless
idols and become worthless
themselves.

Jeremiah 10:2-5 . . . . .God says not to be terrified by
the signs (horoscopes) in the
sky. The customs of the people
are worthless. Idols are like a
scarecrow in a melon patch

Ezekiel 8:14-16 . . . . .Women worship Tammuz (the
plant god) and the men bow
down and face the east as they
worship the sun.

Ezekiel 16:17 . . . . .Idol worship is prostitution
against God.

Acts 19:27-31 . . . . .The people of Ephesus believe
in idols and false gods such as
Artemis of the Ephesians.

Romans 1:25 . . . . .Humanity exchanges the truth of
God for a lie and worship and
serve created things rather than
the Creator.

1 Peter 4:3 . . . . The people are warned not to do
what the pagans choose to do by
living in debauchery, lust,
drunkenness, orgies, carousing,
and detestable idolatry.

1 John 5:21 . . . . Keep yourselves from idols.

Revelation 21:8 . . . . The cowardly, the unbelieving,
the vile, the murderers, the sexu-
ally immoral, those who practice
magical arts, the idolaters and
all liars have their place in fiery
lake of burning sulfur (hell).
This is the second death.

IMMORTALITY

2 Kings 2:11 . . . . A chariot of fire appears and
Elijah is taken up to heaven in a
whirlwind.

Luke 16:19-31 . . . . Jesus tells His disciples the story
about a beggar named Lazarus
(not the same Lazarus that He
raised from the dead) and a rich
man. The rich man dies and
goes to hell where he is in torment in a fire.

John 3:1 . . . . For God so loves the world that
he gave his one and only Son,
that whoever believes in him
shall not perish but have eternal
life.

John 11:25-26 . . . . Jesus is the resurrection and the
life.

Romans 2:16 . . . . .God will judge men's secrets
through Jesus Christ.

1 Corinthians 15:35-49 . .The earthly body is different
from the heavenly body. The
body that dies is perishable, but
it is raised imperishable.

Philippians 1:22-24 . . . . .Paul prefers to be out of the
body and with Christ, which is
better by far. But he must serve
Jesus Christ while in his body.

Hebrews 10:34-35 . . . . . .If we persevere, better things are
waiting for us in eternity.

Revelation 2:11 . . . . .He who overcomes will not be
hurt by the second death (hell).

JESUS

Matthew 1:18-25 . . . . . . .The birth of Jesus, conceived in
Mary through the Holy Spirit.

Matthew 4:23-25 . . . . . . .Jesus heals the sick.

Matthew 5:17 . . . . .Jesus comes to fulfill the law.

Matthew 8:1-4 . . . . .Jesus heals a man with leprosy
(see Mark 1:40-45; Luke 5:12-14).

Matthew 8:14-17 . . . . . . .Jesus heals many people, including Peter's mother-in-law (see
Mark 1:29-34).

Matthew 8:23-27 . . . . . . .Jesus calms the storm.

Matthew 8:28-34 . . . . . . .Jesus cast out demons from two
possessed men. The demons ask
to be sent into a herd of pigs.
Jesus says, "Go." Then the pigs
run off the cliff into a lake and die

Matthew 9:18-26 . . . . . . .Jesus heals a bleeding woman
and restores the life of a girl
who has died (see Mark 5:25-
34; Luke 8:42-56).

Matthew 14:13-21 . . . . . .Jesus feeds five thousand men
besides women and children
with five loaves of bread and
two fish (see Mark 6:30-44.
Luke 9:10-17).

Matthew 14:22-32 . . . . . .Jesus walks on water (see Mark
6:45-52; John 6:16-21).

Matthew 15:29-38 . . . . . .Jesus feeds four thousand men
besides women and children
with seven loaves of bread and a
few small fish (see Mark 8:1-9).

Matthew 17:14-18 . . . . . .Jesus heals an epileptic boy (see
Mark 9:14-27; Luke 9:37-43).

Matthew 17:24-27 . . . . . .Jesus tells Peter to throw his
fishing line into the water and
the first fish he catches will have
a four-drachma coin to pay the
taxes for Him and Peter.

Matthew 20:29-34 . . . . . .Jesus heals two blind men.

Matthew 21:18-22 . . . . . .Jesus puts a curse on a fig tree
and it withers immediately (see
Mark 11:12-14, 20-21).

Matthew 28:1-10 . . . . . . .Jesus is resurrected (see Mark
16:1-8; Luke 24:1-7; John 20:1-
9).

Mark 5:40-43 . . . . .Jesus restores a twelve-year-old
girl to life.

John 8:56-59 . . . . .Jesus acknowledges that He
knew Abraham and before
Abraham was born, He was.

John 10:30 . . . . .Jesus and the Father are one.

John 11:38-44 . . . . .Jesus raises Lazarus, who has
been dead four days, from the
dead.

John 14:2 . . . . .God's house has many rooms.
Jesus goes there to prepare a
place for believers.

John 17:3-5 . . . . .Eternal life and Jesus exist
before the world began.

John 17:24 . . . . .God loves Jesus before the creation of the world.

Acts 1:9   . . . . .The apostles watch as Jesus is
taken up before their very eyes to
heaven.

Philippians 2:5-11 . . . . . .God exalts Jesus.

Colossians 1:15-19 . . . . .Christ is the image of God. He
is the creator.

Hebrews 1:10 . . . . .In the beginning Jesus lays the
foundation of the earth.

Hebrews 4:14-15 . . . . . . .Paul acknowledges that Jesus is
the Son of God.

Revelation 17:14 . . . . . . .Jesus is Lord of Lords and
Kings of Kings.

JUDAS ISCARIOT

Matthew 26:14-16 . . . . . .Judas plans to betray Jesus.

Matthew 26:23-25 . . . . . .Jesus predicts his betrayal by Judas Iscariot (see John 13:21-30).

Matthew 27:3-5 . . . . .Judas returns the thirty silver coins to the chief priests and elders. Then hangs himself.

Matthew 27:6-10 . . . . . . .The chief priests use the thirty pieces of silver to buy the pot- ters' field as a burial place. That is why it is called the Field of Blood.

Mark 3:14-19 . . . . .The twelve apostles are listed. They include Judas Iscariot, who betrayed Jesus.

Luke 22:3 . . . . .Satan enters Judas.

Luke 22:47-48 . . . . .Jesus asks Judas if he is betray- ing the Son of Man.

John 18:2-5 . . . . .Judas guides the soldiers and officials for the arrest of Jesus.

Acts 1:18-19 . . . . .Judas' hangs himself. His body bursts open, and his intestines spills out.

Acts 1:21-26 . . . . .Matthias replaces Judas as an apostle. He is chosen by draw- ing lots.

JUDGMENT, GOD'S

Genesis 3:1-24 . . . . .The fall of man, God's judgment against Satan, God expels man and woman from the Garden of Eden.

Genesis 20:18 . . . . .The Lord temporarily closes up every womb in the household of Abimelech because of his desire for Sarah.

1 Kings 13:1-6 . . . . .King Jeroboam reaches his hand out against the man of God, and his hand shrivels up. God later restores the king's hand.

2 Chronicles 16:10-13 . . .King Asa oppresses his people. His reign ends when he develops an illness. He fails to seek help from the Lord and sought help only from physicians, so he dies.

2 Chronicles 26:16-20 . . .King Uzziah becomes powerful, but his pride leads to his illness. God inflicts leprosy on his forehead.

2 Chronicles 32:24-26 . . .King Hezekiah's heart is proud and he does not respect God's will. He becomes ill, prays to the Lord and repents. Thus, the Lord's wrath does not come upon him.

Psalm 35:4-9 . . . . .King David asks for God's judgment for those who plan to harm him.

Psalm 62:12 . . . . .Each person will be rewarded for what he has done.

Isaiah 1:11-15 . . . . .God rejects the Israelites offerings, incense, meaningless prayers, and rituals.

Jeremiah 5:12-13 . . . . . . .The Israelites think God will not judge them.

Ezekiel 4:12-13 . . . . .God instructs Ezekiel to bake a barley cake using human excrement for fuel, so the people of Israel will eat defiled food in the nations where God will drive them.

Ezekiel 4:14-15 . . . . .God relents to Ezekiel's plea and lets him cook the food over cow manure instead of human excrement.

Ezekiel 9:3-11 . . . . .God puts a mark on the forehead of the righteous in Jerusalem and kills the unbelievers who do not have His mark. He shows no mercy to the men, women, and children without the mark.

Ezekiel 24:15-24 . . . . . . .God takes Ezekiel's wife in death as a sign to the Israelites that the Lord is about to judge them.

Daniel 5:1-30 . . . . .King Belshazzar (King Nebuchadnezzar's son) is not loyal to God, so human fingers appear and write on the wall that he is finished as king. That night he is killed.

Hosea 1:2-5 . . . . .God instructs Hosea to marry an adulterous wife because the land is guilty of the vilest adultery in departing from the Lord.

2 Timothy 3:1-5 . . . . .The last days will have terrible times. People will have a form of godliness but deny its power.

2 Timothy 4:3-4 . . . . .The time will come when men will abandon sound judgment.

Hebrews 9:27 . . . . .Man is destined to die (physically) once and after that to face judgment.

Hebrews 11:29 . . . . .By faith the Hebrews pass through the parted Red Sea, but when the Egyptians try it, they perish.

1 Peter 5:5 . . . . .God opposes the proud but gives grace to the humble.

2 Peter 3:7 . . . . .The Day of Judgment is coming. The present heavens and earth are reserved for fire.

Revelation 3:16 . . . . .The Lord tells the church in Laodicea that if they are lukewarm for Christ—neither hot nor cold—He will spit them out of His mouth.

LANGUAGES

Genesis 11:1 . . . . .The whole world has one language and a common speech.

Genesis 11:7-9 . . . . .The Lord confuses the language of men so they will not understand each other. He scatters them over all the earth. The tower is called *Babel* because

the Lord confuses the language
of all the earth.

Matthew 12:34-35 . . . . . .The mouth speaks from the
overflow of the heart. The good
man brings good things out of
the good stored up in him, and
the evil man brings evil things
out of him.

Matthew 15:11, 18 . . . . . .What goes into a man's mouth
does not make him unclean, but
what comes out of his mouth
makes him unclean (see
Ephesians 4:29, 5:4).

Acts 2:1-12 . . . . .The Holy Spirit enables people
to understand each other's lan-
guage on the Day of Pentecost.

Colossians 3:8 . . . . .We must rid ourselves of anger,
rage, malice, slander, and filthy
language from our lips.

Colossians 4:6 . . . . .Let your conversations be
always full of grace and sea-
soned with salt.

LAWSUITS

Exodus 23:2-3 . . . . .Do not pervert justice by siding
with the crowd, and do not show
favoritism to a poor man in his
lawsuit.

Proverbs 25:8 . . . . .Do not be in a hurry to go to
court.

Hosea 10:4 . . . . .Worldly people will make many promises, take false oaths, and make agreements. Therefore lawsuits spring up like poisonous weeds in a plowed field.

Amos 5:15 . . . . .Maintain justice in the courts.

Matthew 5:25 . . . . .Settle matters quickly with your adversary who is taking you to court.

1 Corinthians 6:1-6 . . . . .Settle disputes among yourselves within the church. Do not take your problems before the ungodly.

1 Corinthians 6:7-8 . . . . .Your lawsuits against other Christians mean you are completely defeated already.

LIFE SPAN

Genesis 5:5 . . . . .Adam lives 930 years, then he dies.

Genesis 5:8 . . . . .Seth (Adam's son) lives 912 years, then he dies.

Genesis 5:20 . . . . .Jared lives 962 years, then he dies.

Genesis 5:23-24 . . . . . . .Enoch (father of Methuselah) walks with God. God took him away to heaven at 365 years.

Genesis 5:27 . . . . .Methuselah lives 969 years, then he dies.

Genesis 5:32 . . . . .After Noah is 500 years old, he becomes the father of Shem, Ham, and Japheth. Noah lives 950 years, then he dies (see Genesis 9:28).

Genesis 6:3 . . . . .God shortens man's days to 120 years.

Genesis 7:6 . . . . .Noah is 600 years old when the floodwaters come on earth.

Genesis 23:1-2 . . . . .Sarah is 127 years old when she dies. She is 90 years old when she gives birth to Isaac (see Genesis 17:17-19).

Genesis 25:7-8 . . . . .Abraham is 175 years old when he dies, and he is gathered to his people. Abraham is 100 years old when he fathers Isaac (see Genesis 17:17-19).

Genesis 35:28 . . . . .Isaac lives 180 years.

Exodus 7:7 . . . . .Moses is 80 years old and Aaron 83 when they speak to Pharaoh.

Deuteronomy 32:48-52 . .God tells Moses to go up to Mount Nebo in Moab and there he will die and be gathered to his people, because Moses and his brother Aaron both broke faith with God in the presence of the Israelites at the waters of Meribah-kadesh.

Deuteronomy 34:5-7 . . . .The Lord buries Moses. No one knows where his grave is. Moses is 120 years old when he dies. His eyes are not weak nor his strength gone.

Joshua 24:29 . . . . .Joshua dies at 110 years of age.

2 Samuel 14:14 . . . . .We must all die eventually, like water spilled on the ground that cannot be recovered.

Job 42:16 . . . . .Job lives 140 years, then he dies, an old man and full of years.

Psalm 89:48 . . . . .Man cannot save himself from the power of the grave.

Psalm 90:10 . . . . .Our days are seventy or eighty years, if we have the strength. Yet their span is but trouble and sorrow, for they quickly pass and we fly away.

LIFTING HANDS/PRAISE

2 Chronicles 6:12-13 . . . .Solomon raises his hands in prayer when standing and kneeling.

Psalm 134:2 . . . . .Lift up your hands in the sanctuary and praise the Lord.

Psalm 150:6 . . . . .Let everything that lives praise the Lord.

1 Peter 1:3 . . . . .Praise be to the God and Father of our Lord Jesus Christ, who gives us hope through the resurrection of Jesus Christ from the dead.

1 Peter 4:16 . . . . .If you suffer as a Christian, do
                              not be ashamed, but praise God
                              that you bear that name.

Revelation 5:13 . . . . . . .Every creature in heaven and on
                              earth and under the earth and on
                              the sea sings praises to the Lord.

MARRIAGE

Genesis 2:24 . . . . .Man will leave his father and
                              mother and be united with his
                              wife, and they will become one
                              flesh.

Deuteronomy 7:3-4 . . . . .Believers must not marry
                              pagans.

Deuteronomy 17:17 . . . . .Man must not take many wives
                              or his heart will be led astray.

1 Kings 11:1-13 . . . . . . .Solomon marries pagan wives
                              contrary to the will of the Lord.
                              He has seven hundred wives and
                              three hundred concubines. His
                              wives lead him astray by turning
                              his heart after other gods.

Proverbs 19:13 . . . . .A quarrelsome wife is like a
                              constant dripping.

Proverbs 21:9 . . . . .Better to live on the corner of
                              the roof than with a quarrelsome
                              wife (see Proverbs 25:24).

Proverbs 21:19 . . . . .Better to live in a desert than
                              with a quarrelsome wife.

Proverbs 27:15-16 . . . . . .A quarrelsome wife is like a
                              constant dripping on a rainy day.

Restraining her is like restraining the wind or grasping oil with the hand.

Jeremiah 16:1-4 . . . . .God tells Jeremiah not to marry in Jerusalem, because the people will die of deadly diseases and their dead bodies will become food for the birds of the air and beasts of the earth.

Matthew 5:32 . . . . .Anyone who divorces their spouse, except for marital unfaithfulness, causes them to commit adultery, and anyone who marries a person so divorced commits adultery.

Matthew 19:5-6 . . . . .God joins together a husband and wife. Let no one separate them.

Mark 12:25 . . . . .There will be no marriage in heaven. People will be like the angels in heaven.

Luke 20:34-36 . . . . .Jesus says there will be no marriage in heaven.

Romans 7:2-3 . . . . .Marriage after the death of a spouse is permissible.

1 Corinthians 7:3-5 . . . . .Husbands and wives should not deprive each other sexually.

1 Corinthians 7:8-9 . . . . .It is good if unmarried people can stay unmarried, but it is better to marry than burn with passion.

1 Corinthians 7:10-11 . . . Husbands and wives should not separate from one another.

1 Corinthians 7:28 . . . . . . Those who marry will face many troubles in this life.

1 Corinthians 7:38 . . . . . . Better not to marry.

1 Corinthians 7:39 . . . . . If you are to get married, you must marry a Christian.

2 Corinthians 6:14 . . . . . Do not be yoked together with unbelievers.

Ephesians 5:22-24 . . . . . . Wives, submit to your husbands, for the husband is the head of the wife as Christ is the head of the church.

Ephesians 5:25 . . . . Husbands, love your wives, just as Christ loves the church.

Hebrews 13:4 . . . . The marriage bed should be kept pure.

1 Peter 3:1-5 . . . . Wives, submit to your husbands.

MEN

Genesis 1:26-27 . . . . God creates man in his own image and likeness, and man will have dominion over all the earth. In the image of God he creates him. Male and female he creates them.

Genesis 2:7 . . . . The Lord God forms man from the dust of the ground and breathes into his nostrils the breath of life.

Genesis 2:19-20 . . . . .The Lord God forms all animals
out of the ground and brings
them to Adam to name. So
Adam gives names to all livestock, birds, and beasts.

Genesis 9:6 . . . . .Whoever sheds the blood of
man, by man shall his blood be
shed. Man is made in God's
image.

Job 5:7 . . . . .Man is born for trouble as surely
as sparks fly upward.

Job 10:9 . . . . .God molds man like clay and
will return him to dust again.

Job 13:28 . . . . .Man wastes away like something rotten.

Psalm 8:5 . . . . .God makes man a little lower
than the heavenly beings and
crowns him with glory and
honor (see Hebrews 2:7).

Ecclesiastes 1:11 . . . . . . .Man will not be remembered.

Romans 5:12-19 . . . . . . .Sin and death enters the world
through Adam. Death comes to
all people, because everyone has
sinned. Jesus brings forgiveness
of sin for those who believe and
accept Him.

Ephesians 5:25 . . . . .Husbands, love your wives, just
as Christ loves the church.

MIRACLES

Genesis 5:21-24 . . . . .God takes Enoch away to heaven (see Hebrews 11:5).

Exodus 8:16-19 . . . . .The Lord tells Moses to say to Aaron to stretch out his staff and strike the dust of the earth that gnats might swarm throughout Egypt.

Exodus 8:20-24 . . . . .The Lord brings flies on the land of Egypt, but not on the Israelites. God spares His people.

Exodus 9:1-7 . . . . .The Lord brings a plague upon the Egyptians and kills all of their animals. None of the animals of the Israelites were harmed.

Exodus 9:8-12 . . . . .The Lord brings boils to the Egyptians and their animals.

Exodus 9:18-26 . . . . .God sends the worst hailstorm since Egypt was founded. No Israelites were harmed.

Exodus 10:4-18 . . . . .The Lord brings the worst plague of locusts to Egypt.

Exodus 11:4-10 . . . . .The Lord kills the firstborn son of the Egyptians as well as the firstborn of the cattle.

Exodus 12:4-30 . . . ."The Passover." The Lord tells Moses to have the Israelites kill lambs and spread the blood on the sides and tops of the doorframes so when He comes in the night, He will see the blood and pass over His people and no destructive plague will touch the Israelites.

Exodus 13:18-22 . . . . . . .God leads the Israelites out of Egypt. He goes ahead in a pillar of cloud by day and a pillar of fire by night, which never leaves its place in front of the people.

Exodus 14:16 . . . . .God instructs Moses to raise his staff and stretch out his hand over the sea to divide the water so the Israelites can go through the divided sea on dry ground.

Exodus 14:19-20 . . . . . . .Then the pillar of cloud by day and pillar of fire by night was moved from in front and stood behind them, coming between the armies of Egypt and Israel. Through the night the cloud brought darkness to the Egyptians and light to the Israelites.

Exodus 14:21-22 . . . . . . .Moses stretches out his hand over the sea, and all that night the Lord drives the sea back with a strong east wind and turns it into dry land.

Exodus 14:25 . . . . .God causes the wheels of the Egyptian chariots to swerve while they are chasing the Israelites.

Exodus 14:26-30 . . . . . . .God lets the parted waters of the sea flow back and kills all of the Egyptian army. Not one of them survives.

Exodus 15:22-25 . . . . . . .God uses a piece of wood to sweeten the drinking water in the desert.

Exodus 16:10-36 . . . . . . .God provides manna (bread) from heaven and quail for the Israelites to eat. They eat manna for forty years.

Exodus 17:1-7 . . . . .The Lord has Moses use his staff to strike the rock at Horeb, and water comes out for the people to drink.

Numbers 22:21-34 . . . . . .Balaam beats his donkey and the donkey speaks to him (see Numbers 22:30). The Lord opens Balaam's eyes to see the angel of the Lord. The donkey has already seen the angel.

Joshua 3:13 . . . . .God piles up in a heap the waters of the Jordan River.

Joshua 3:14-17 . . . . .The priests carrying the Ark of the Covenant stand on dry ground in the middle of the river, which is at flood stage during harvest, while the Israelites passes through.

Joshua 4:18 . . . . .God allows the waters of the Jordan River to start flowing again once the Israelites are across.

Joshua 4:22-24 . . . . .God divides the Jordan River as He did the Red Sea.

Joshua 5:12 . . . . .God stops the manna from heaven when the Israelites eat the produce of the land of Canaan.

Joshua 6:2-26 . . . . .God tells Joshua how to destroy Jericho, and the walls collapse.

Joshua 10:12-14 . . . . . . .God stops the sun from going down for a full day in response to Joshua's request.

Judges 13:1-25 . . . . .The angel of the Lord tells Manoah's wife that she will have a son (Samson) who will begin the deliverance of Israel from the Philistines.

Judges 14:5-6 . . . . .Samson kills a young lion with his bare hands. He tares the lion apart like a goat.

Judges 15:13-16 . . . . . . .Samson kills one thousand Philistines with the jawbone of a donkey.

1 Samuel 5:1-5 . . . . .The statue of the Philistine god, Dagon, fell on its face before the Ark of the Covenant, which the Philistines had captured.

1 Samuel 6:19-20 . . . . . .God kills seventy Philistine men for looking inside the Ark of the Covenant.

2 Kings 4:32-37 . . . . .Elisha prays to God and brings a young boy back to life.

2 Kings 5:9-15 . . . . .Elisha tells Naaman who has leprosy to wash himself seven times   in the Jordan, and he will be cured.

2 Kings 6:5-7 . . . . .Elisha floats an iron ax head.

2 Kings 7:6-7 . . . . .The Lord causes the Arameans to hear the sound of horses and chariots, so they flee.

2 Kings 13:20-21 . . . . . . .The body of a dead man is thrown into Elisha's tomb. When the body touches Elisha's bones, the man comes to life and stands up.

2 Kings 19:35 . . . . .The angel of the Lord kills 185,000 men in the Assyrian camp (see 2 Chronicles 32:20-21, Isaiah 37:36-37).

2 Kings 20:1-7 . . . . .The Lord adds fifteen years to the life of King Hezekiah.

2 Kings 20:8-11 . . . . . . .The Lord gives King Hezekiah a sign that He will heal him. The shadow cast by the sun goes back ten steps (see Isaiah 38:1-8)

2 Chronicles 1:8-12 . . . . .King Solomon asks God for wisdom. This wish is granted plus riches as well.

Isaiah 48:21 . . . . .God splits a rock in the desert, and water gushes from it.

the animals and eat grass like
cattle. His hair will grow like
the feathers of an eagle, and he
will have nails like the claws of
a bird. His sanity is restored and
he worships the one true God.

Daniel 6:6-28 . . . . .King Darius throws Daniel into
a den of lions. Daniel is not
harmed. His accusers and their
wives and children are thrown
into the den, and their bones are
crushed.

Jonah 1:4-16 . . . . .The events of Jonah in the ship
on the way to Tarshish are
described. Jonah is running
away from God and a violent
storm strikes the ship he was in.
Jonah tells the sailors to throw
him into the water. When they
do the seas become calm.

Jonah 1:17 . . . . .The Lord provides a great fish to
swallow Jonah. He is inside the
fish three days and three nights.

Jonah 2:10 . . . . .The Lord commands the fish,
and it vomits Jonah onto dry
land.

Jonah 3:1-10 . . . . .Jonah goes to Nineveh and God
spares the city.

Matthew 14:13-21 . . . . .Jesus feeds five thousand men,
besides women and children,
with five loaves of bread and
two fish (see Mark 6:30-44,
Luke 9:10-17).

John 4:43-54 . . . . .Jesus restores an official's son back to life (Jesus' second recorded miracle on earth).

John 5:1-8 . . . . .Jesus heals a man who has been crippled for thirty-eight years.

John 11:38-44 . . . . .Jesus raises Lazarus from the dead.

Acts 3:1-10 . . . . .Peter heals a crippled beggar.

Acts 12:1-10 . . . . .An angel of the Lord helps Peter escape from prison.

MONEY/WEALTH

Genesis 13:2 . . . . .Abram becomes very wealthy in livestock, silver, and gold.

Exodus 22:21-25 . . . . . .Do not mistreat an alien, and do not charge interest on money loaned to one of God's people.

1 Kings 10:14 . . . . .Solomon receives about 25 tons of gold each year (see 2 Chronicles 9:13-28).

Job 31:24-28 . . . . .The worship of money is unfaithfulness to God.

Psalm 39:6 . . . . .Man heaps up wealth not knowing who will get it.

Psalm 49:10-13 . . . . . . .Wise and foolish men alike perish and leave their wealth to others. Man does not endure. Do not trust in yourself..

show restraint. Cast but a glance at riches, and they are gone, for they will surely sprout wings and fly off to the sky like an eagle.

Proverbs 27:24 . . . . .Riches do not endure forever, and a crown is not secure for all generations.

Proverbs 30:8-9 . . . . .Ask for neither poverty nor riches, but ask only for daily bread. Otherwise, you may have too much and disown the Lord or become poor and steal and so dishonor God.

Ecclesiastes 1:3-4 . . . . . .What does man gain from all his labor? Generations come and go, but the earth remains forever.

Ecclesiastes 5:10-12 . . . .Whoever loves money never has enough. Whoever loves wealth is never satisfied with his income. This is meaningless.

Luke 12:15 . . . . .Be on your guard against all kinds of greed. A mans life does not consist in the abundance of his possessions.

Luke 12:22-31 . . . . .Do not worry about your life, what you will eat or wear or about your body. Life is more than food and clothes.

Luke 12:34 . . . . .For where your treasure is, there your heart will be also.

Luke 16:13 . . . . .No servant can serve two mas-
ters. You cannot serve both God
and Money.

Luke 21:1-4 . . . . .A poor widow's offering of two
small copper coins is all she has
to live on. Jesus considers it
greater than all the other
offerings.

1 Timothy 6:7 . . . . .We brought nothing into this
world, and we can take nothing
out of it.

1 Timothy 6:9 . . . . .People who want to get rich fall
into temptation and a trap and
into many foolish harmful
desires that plunge men into ruin
and destruction.

1 Timothy 6:10 . . . . .For the love of money is a root
of all kinds of evil.

Hebrews 13:5 . . . . .Keep your lives free from the
love of money and be content
with what you have, because
God says, "I will never leave
you nor forsake you."

James 5:1-6 . . . . .The Lord warns the rich oppres-
sors who mistreat others.

NAMES, BIBLICAL

Genesis 14:18-20 . . . . . .Melchizedek is the King of
Salem (Jerusalem) and is priest
of God Most High. He blesses
Abram.

Judges 3:16-30 . . . . .Ehud uses a sword about one and a half feet long and plunges it into King Eglon's belly. The handle sinks in after the blade and his fat closes in over the sword.

Judges 3:31 . . . . .Shamgar strikes down six hundred Philistines with an oxgoad.

Judges 6:11-23 . . . . .Gideon is chosen by the angel of the Lord to save Israel. Gideon is very reluctant.

Judges 13:1-25 . . . . .The angel of the Lord tells Manoah's wife that she will have a son (Samson) who will begin the deliverance of Israel from the Philistines.

1 Samuel 17:4-7 . . . . . . .Goliath is a Philistine over nine feet tall. He wears a coat of bronze scale armor weighing about 125 pounds. The iron point of his spear weighs 15 pounds.

1 Samuel 17:40 . . . . .Young David picks five smooth stones from the stream to fight Goliath.

1 Samuel 17:48-51 . . . . .Young David kills Goliath with a single stone, then he cut off Goliath's head.

1 Samuel 21:12-15 . . . . .David intentionally acts like a madman to save his life in the presence of King Achish of Gath.

1 Samuel 24:3-7 . . . . . . .David spares King Saul's life
while Saul is relieving himself
in a cave. David crept up unno-
ticed and cut off a corner of
Saul's robe.

2 Samuel 6:16, 23 . . . . . .Michal, daughter of Saul,
despises David. She remains
childless to the day of her death.

2 Samuel 12:24 . . . . . . .King David and Bathsheba have
a second son named Solomon.

2 Samuel 18:9-17 . . . . . .The long hair of Absalom, son
of King David, is caught in the
branches of a tree. King David's
commander, Joab, stabs him to
death.

2 Samuel 21:20 . . . . . . .David's brother kills a huge man
with six fingers on each hand
and six toes on each foot.

1 Kings 2:6-9 . . . . .King David tells Solomon to kill
two of his adversaries. "Do not
let his gray head go down to the
grave in peace."

2 Kings 11:21 . . . . .Joash is seven years old when he
becomes king.

2 Kings 14:25 . . . . .Jonah is first mentioned.

2 Kings 17:23 . . . . .The Lord exiles the Israelites to
Assyria.

2 Kings 18:11-12 . . . . . .The Israelites are exiled to
Assyria because they fail to
obey God's commands.

1 Chronicles 11:22-25 . . . Benaiah kills a lion and a large Egyptian who is seven and one half feet tall. He went against the Egyptian with a club, snatches the spear from the Egyptian's hand, and kills him with his own spear.

2 Chronicles 9:1-12 . . . . . The queen of Sheba visits King Solomon.

Isaiah 10:20 . . . . The word *remnant* refers to a number of survivors of God's wrath.

Ezekiel 4:4-8 . . . . God instructs Ezekiel to lie on his side for a total of four hundred and thirty days (the number of days the Israelites are in captivity). This is 390 days to bear the punishment of the house of Israel and forty days to bear the punishment of the house of Judah.

Amos 7:14-15 . . . . Amos has humble beginnings. When God calls him, Amos has no special training.

Jonah 4:11 . . . . Nineveh has more than 120,000 people who cannot tell their right hand from their left.

Matthew 2:3 . . . . King Herod is disturbed by the news of the birth of Jesus.

Luke 6:13-16 . . . . The twelve apostles are Simon (Peter), Andrew, James, John, Philip, Bartholomew, Matthew,

Thomas, James (son of
Alphaeus), Simon (called the
Zealot), Judas (son of James)
and Judas Iscariot (the traitor).

Acts 23:7-8 . . . . .The difference between the
Pharisees and the Sadducees is
that the Sadducees do not
believe in any type of resurrection, angels, or spirits and the
Pharisees acknowledge them all.

Hebrews 5:6-10 . . . . . . .God compares Jesus to
Melchizedek.

Hebrews 7:1-3 . . . . .Melchizedek, King of Salem
(Jerusalem) and priest of God
Most High, has no father or
mother and no genealogy. He is
without beginning of days or
end of life. Like the Son of God
he remains a priest forever.

PAUL, APOSTLE

Acts 8:1-3 . . . . .Saul (later called Paul) perse-
cutes the church.

Acts 9:1-19 . . . . .Jesus temporarily blinds Saul
(later called Paul, see Acts 13:9),
on the road to Damascus and he
becomes a believer (see Acts
22:6-13).

Acts 14:19-20 . . . . .Paul is stoned but not killed.

2 Corinthians 11:23-27 . . .Paul suffers for Christ. He is flogged five times with thirty-nine lashes each time.

2 Corinthians 12:2-4 . . . .Paul refers to his being caught up to the third heaven where he hears inexpressible things that God will not permit him to tell.

2 Corinthians 12:7-10 . . .Paul is given a thorn in the flesh to keep him from becoming conceited because of his knowledge of surpassingly great revelations.

Galatians 1:1 . . . . .Paul an apostle, sent not from men nor man, but from Jesus Christ and God the Father, who raises Him from the dead.

Galatians 1:11 . . . . .The gospel does not come from man. Paul receives it by revelation from Jesus Christ.

Galatians 1:15-16 . . . . . .God set Paul apart from birth.

Galatians 1:17-18 . . . . . .Paul went to Arabia after his conversion.

Galatians 2:7 . . . . .Peter has been given the task of preaching the gospel to the Jews and Paul the task of preaching the gospel to the Gentiles.

Ephesians 3:7-11 . . . . . .Paul's mission is to preach to the Gentiles.

Colossians 1:1 . . . . .Paul, an apostle of Christ Jesus by the will of God.

1 Thessalonians 3:3-4 . . .Apostle Paul states that believers will be persecuted.

1 Timothy 1:13 ....Paul is a blasphemer, a persecu-
tor, and a violent man.

PENTECOST

Acts 2:1 ....When the day of Pentecost came
(the day the disciples receive the
Holy Spirit), the disciples are all
together in one place.

Acts 2:2 ....Suddenly a sound like the blow-
ing of a violent wind comes
from heaven and fills the whole
house where the apostles are
sitting.

Acts 2:3 ....They see what seems to be
tongues of fire that separate and
come to rest on each of the
apostles.

Acts 2:4 ....All of the apostles are filled with
the Holy Spirit and begin to
speak in other tongues (lan-
guages) as the Spirit enables
them.

PETER, APOSTLE

Matthew 14:28-31 ......Peter walks on water to Jesus in
the Sea of Galilee.

Matthew 16:13-17 ......God reveals to Peter that Jesus is
the Christ, the son of the living
God.

Matthew 16:18 ....Jesus tells Peter (which means
rock), "You are Peter and upon

this rock (his faith and confession in Jesus Christ) I will build My church, and the gates of Hades (hell) will not overcome it."

Matthew 17:1-4 . . . . .Jesus takes Peter, James, and John up a high mountain where Jesus is transfigured before them. Moses and Elijah appear and they are talking with Jesus.

Luke 5:1-11 . . . . .The calling of the first disciples. Jesus provides a large catch of fish for Simon Peter, who confesses that he is a sinner. Jesus says, "Don't be afraid, from now on you will catch men."

Luke 22:55-62 . . . . .Peter denies knowing Jesus three times. Then the rooster crows as predicted.

Acts 4:13 . . . . .Peter and John are unschooled, ordinary men.

Acts 9:36-41 . . . . .Peter restores Tabitha (Dorcas) back to life.

Acts 12:5-11 . . . . .An angel rescues Peter from prison.

Galatians 2:7 . . . . .Peter is given the task of preaching the gospel to the Jews and Paul the task of preaching the gospel to the Gentiles.

PRAYER

2 Chronicles 7:1-3 . . . . . . When King Solomon finishes praying, fire comes down from heaven. When all the Israelites see the glory of the Lord, they kneel down and worship the Lord.

Psalm 4:1 . . . . King David asks God to answer his call and to give relief from his distress.

Matthew 5:44 . . . . Love your enemies and pray for those who persecute you.

Matthew 6:5-6 . . . . When you pray do not pray in public but rather pray in private.

Matthew 6:7 . . . . When praying do not keep on babbling like pagans using many words.

Matthew 6:9-15 . . . . The Lord's Prayer is Jesus' instructions as to how we should pray: "Our Father in heaven, hallowed be your name, your kingdom come, your will be done on earth as it is in heaven. Give us today our daily bread. Forgive us our debts, as we have forgiven our debtors. And lead us not into temptation, but deliver us from the evil one" (see also Luke 11:2-4).

Luke 22:44-45 . . . . Jesus prays and His sweat is like blood falling to the ground.

When he rose from praying, He finds the disciples asleep, exhausted from sorrow.

John 14:12-14 . . . . .Anyone who has faith in Jesus may ask Jesus for anything in His name, and it will be done.

John 15:16 . . . . .The Father chooses us to bear fruit for Him. The Father will give you whatever you ask in His name.

John 17:1-5 . . . . .Jesus prays for Himself.

John 17:6-19 . . . . .Jesus prays for His disciples.

John 17:20-26 . . . . .Jesus prays for all believers, including present-day believers.

Acts 4:24-31 . . . . .The believers pray for boldness in spreading the Gospel.

Acts 9:10-19 . . . . .The Lord commissions Ananias to go to Saul (also called Paul) who is praying about a vision he has had. Ananias goes to Saul, lays hands on him, and restores his sight.

1 Thessalonians 5:17-18 . .Pray continually gives thanks for all circumstances.

James 5:13 . . . . .If you have trouble, pray.

PRIDE

1 Samuel 2:1-3 . . . . . . .Do not keep talking so proudly or let your mouth speak arrogance, for the Lord knows.

Psalm 10:2-11 . . . . .In their pride the wicked have no room for God.

Proverbs 16:18 . . . . . . .Pride goes before destruction, a haughty spirit before a fall.

Proverbs 18:11-12 . . . . . .Before his downfall a man's heart is proud, but humility comes before honor.

Proverbs 21:24 . . . . .The proud and arrogant man, "Mocker" is his name. He behaves with great pride.

Jeremiah 48:29 . . . . . . .Moab has pride and arrogance and haughtiness of heart.

Daniel 4:37 . . . . .King Nebuchadnezzar states that those who walk in pride God is able to humble.

Mark 12:38-40 . . . . .Proud teachers of the law and their ungodly behavior.

Acts 12:19-23 . . . . .The cost of Herod's pride: An angel of the Lord strikes him down, and worms eat him.

1 Corinthians 13:4 . . . . . .Love does not envy, does not boast, is not proud.

2 Corinthians 11:30 . . . . .Apostle Paul boasts only of things that show his weakness.

2 Corinthians 12:7-10 . . .Apostle Paul is given a thorn in the flesh to prevent him from becoming conceited.

1 Timothy 3:6 . . . . .A Christian leader must not be a recent convert, or he may become conceited.

Galatians 6:3 . . . . .If anyone thinks he is something
when he is nothing, he deceives
himself.

2 Timothy 3:1-5 . . . . . . .In the last days people will be
lovers of themselves, lovers of
money, boastful, proud, abusive,
disobedient to their parents,
ungrateful and unholy. Have
nothing to do with them.

James 4:6 . . . . .God opposes the proud but gives
grace to the humble.

1 Peter 5:5-6 . . . . .God opposes the proud but gives
grace to the humble.

1 John 2:16 . . . . .The cravings of sinful man
include the boasting of what he
does. This comes not from the
Father but from the world.

PROMISED LAND

Genesis 17:7-8 . . . . .The Lord makes a covenant with
Abraham (God changes his
name from Abram) and his
descendants to give them the
land of Canaan.

Deuteronomy 6:10-12 . . .The Promised Land given to the
Israelites already have large
flourishing cities, so even
though the Israelites did not
build, they had houses filled
with all kinds of good things
already provided, wells they did

not dig and vineyards and olive groves already planted.

Deuteronomy 7:1 . . . . . . .God drives out seven larger Canaanite nations so His people could occupy the land.

Deuteronomy 7:2-6 . . . . .God orders the Israelites to destroy the Canaanite nations totally and show them no mercy. They are also not to intermarry with them, for they will turn them away from following God to serve other gods.

Deuteronomy 7:16 . . . . . .God again tells the Israelites that they must destroy all the Canaanite people the Lord gives over to them.

Joshua 3:10 . . . . .The tribes that God drives out of the Promised Land for the Israelites are the Canaanites, Hittites, Hivites, Perizzites, Girgashites, Amorites, and Jebusites.

Joshua 3:13-14 . . . . .God parts the Jordan at flood stage and piles the water up in a heap so the Israelites can cross into the Promised Land.

Joshua 3:15-17 . . . . .As soon as the priests carrying the Ark of the Covenant touches the waters of the Jordan, God parts the waters and they stand on dry, firm ground in the middle of the Jordan.

Joshua 4:18 . . . . .The waters of the Jordan begin
flowing again as soon as the
priests carrying the Ark of the
Covenant set their feet on dry
ground.

Joshua 4:22-24 . . . . .God did to the Jordan what He
did to the Red Sea for the
Israelites.

Joshua 5:12 . . . . .God stops the manna from heav-
en the day after the Israelites eat
food from the land of Canaan
(Promised Land).

PROPHECY

Isaiah 7:14 . . . . .The Lord will give a sign: the
virgin will be with child and will
give birth to a son and will call
him Immanuel.

Isaiah 53:1-6 . . . . .Isaiah is describing Christ
(before He is born).

Jeremiah 23:5-6 . . . . . . .Jeremiah prophesies about
Christ's coming (from David's
line).

Micah 5:2 . . . . .Micah prophesies that Israel's
ruler (Christ) will be born in
Bethlehem.

Zechariah 9:9 . . . . .Prediction that Zion's king
(Jesus) will have salvation and
come riding on a donkey.

Matthew 26:2 . . . . .Jesus prophesies His crucifixion
(see Mark 8:31-33)

Matthew 26:31-35 . . . . . .Jesus predicts Peter's denial (see Matthew 26:69-75).

John 13:19-21 . . . . .Jesus prophesies that one of his followers was going to betray Him (A name was not given. We now know that it was Judas Iscariot).

Acts 11:28-30 . . . . .The prophet Agabus predicts through the spirit that a severe famine will spread over the Roman world (this happens during the reign of Claudius).

1 Corinthians 14:1-5 . . . .Paul states that prophesying is of more value than speaking in tongues.

1 Corinthians 14:22 . . . . .Tongues (speaking in) are a sign, not for believers but for unbelievers. Prophecy, however, is for believers, not for unbelievers.

1 Corinthians 14:39 . . . . .Be eager to prophesy, and do not forbid speaking in tongues (see 1 Corinthians 14:27-28).

2 Thessalonians 2:2 . . . . .Do not become easily unsettled or alarmed by some who prophesy that the day of the Lord has already come.

2 Peter 1:20-21 . . . . . . .No prophecy of Scripture comes about by the prophet's own interpretation but rather from God carried along by the Holy Spirit.

Revelation 22:18-19 . . . . If anyone adds or takes away from the book of prophecy (book of Revelation), God will severely punish him.

PROPHETS

Deuteronomy 13:1-5 . . . . If a prophet or one who foretells dreams correctly predicts a future event and invites you to follow other gods, you must not listen to him. The Lord your God is testing you to find out if you love Him.

1 Kings 18:4 . . . . Jezebel kills many of the Lord's prophets.

1 Kings 18:40 . . . . Elijah commands the people to seize the false prophets of Baal and take them to the Kishon Valley and slaughter them.

2 Chronicles 36:15-17 . . . The Lord God sends word to the people in Jerusalem through his messengers and prophets. The people despise and mock them. The wrath of the Lord is aroused so much that he brings up against Jerusalem the Babylonians who kill the Israelites.

Psalm 105:15 . . . . Do not touch my anointed ones. Do my prophets no harm.

Jeremiah 14:14-16 . . . . . . False prophets will perish by the sword.

Jeremiah 23:10-14 . . . . . . .The lying prophets follow an evil course and use their power unjustly. Both prophet and priest are godless.

Micah 3:5-6 . . . . .The Lord says, "As for the prophets who lead my people astray, the sun will set for the prophets."

Matthew 13:57 . . . . .Jesus says, "Only in his home town and in his own house is a prophet without honor."

Matthew 23:37 . . . . .Jesus accuses Jerusalem of killing the prophets and stoning those sent to them.

Matthew 24:11 . . . . .Jesus states that during the end times, many false prophets will appear and deceive many people.

Luke 6:26 . . . . .Woe to you when all men speak well of you, for that is how their fathers treated the false prophets.

John 4:44 . . . . .Jesus Himself has pointed out that a prophet has no honor in his own country.

PUNISHMENTS, GOD'S

Genesis 3:7-18 . . . . .The Lord is unhappy with Adam and Eve because of their sin. He increases childbearing pain for

Eve and curses the ground so
Adam will have painful toil.

Genesis 3:17-19 . . . . .Because Adam listens to his
wife (Eve) and eats from the tree
of life, God curses the ground. It
will produce thorns and thistles.
Man will return to the ground
from which he was taken.

Genesis 38:7 . . . . .The Lord kills Er (Judah's firstborn) because he is wicked in
the Lord's sight.

Genesis 38:8-10 . . . . .Onan, the brother of Er (now
deceased), sleeps with Er's wife
to fulfill his duty as a brother-in-
law to produce offspring for his
brother.

Genesis 38:9-10 . . . . .Onan spills his seed on the
ground when he lay with his
brother's wife so she will not get
pregnant. This is wicked in the
Lord's sight, so He puts Onan to
death.

Exodus 22:10-15 . . . . . . .God's rules dealing with person-
al property, specifically animals.

Exodus 22:18 . . . . .Do not allow a sorceress to live.

Exodus 22:20 . . . . .Whoever sacrifices to any god
other than the Lord must be
destroyed.

Exodus 32:32-35 . . . . . . .God will punish those who sin
against Him. The Lord strikes
the Israelites with a plague

because they worship the golden
calf that Aaron has made.

Leviticus 10:1-3 . . . . .God puts Aaron's sons, Nadab
and Abihu, to death for offering
an unauthorized fire before the
Lord.

Leviticus 24:10-16 . . . . . .If anyone blasphemes (curses)
the name of the Lord, they are to
be put to death.

Leviticus 24:17-20 . . . . . .If anyone takes the life of a
human being, he must be put to
death., Fracture for fracture, eye
for an eye, tooth for tooth.

Numbers 31:15-18 . . . . . .Moses orders the soldiers to kill
all the Midianite boys and all
women who have slept with a
man.

Deuteronomy 2:31-34 . . .The Lord hands King Sihon of
Heshbon over to the Israelites to
be killed along with his sons and
his whole army. God also tells
the Israelites to completely
destroy the towns, including the
men, women, and children.

Deuteronomy 3:3-7 . . . . .The Lord hands Og, King of
Bashan, over to the Israelites to
kill all his army and to completely destroy sixty cities,
including the men, women, and
children.

Deuteronomy 13:1-5 . . . .Do not follow false prophets.
God will test you to see if you

are loyal. Put false prophets to death.

Deuteronomy 13:6-18 . . .If your own brother or son or daughter or wife entices you to worship other gods, you must put him to death. Your hand must be the first in putting him to death.

Deuteronomy 17:5-7 . . . .A person must not be put to death with only one witness. Only on the testimony of two or three witnesses (see Numbers 35:30; Deuteronomy 19:15). The hands of the witnesses must be the first in putting him to death, then the hands of all the people.

Deuteronomy 22:22-29 . .The punishment for sleeping with another man's wife is death for both. The punishment for rape is death.

Deuteronomy 24:7 . . . . . .The punishment for kidnapping is death.

Deuteronomy 28:63-64 . .For disobedience to God, He will scatter the Israelites among all the nations.

Joshua 6:20-21 . . . . .When the Israelites sound the trumpets and give a loud shout, the walls of Jericho fell. Then Joshua and his army kills every living thing in it—men, women, and livestock.

Joshua 12:2-24 . . . . .Joshua and the Israelites kill
thirty-one kings.

Judges 1:4-7 . . . . .God pays back the Canaanite
King Adoni-Bezek by cutting off
his thumbs and toes.

Judges 5:8 . . . . .When Israel chose new gods,
war came to the city gates.

1 Samuel 28:8-19 . . . . . .King Saul consults a medium to
call up Samuel's spirit from the
ground, then Saul converses
with a spirit claiming to be
Samuel's spirit. The spirit states
that since King Saul did not
obey the Lord, David will
replace him and the Lord will
hand King Saul over to the
Philistines.

2 Kings 9:30-37 . . . . .Jezebel is killed and her body
eaten by dogs.

2 Kings 25:8-21 . . . . .The Babylonians capture and
sack Jerusalem.

1 Chronicles 5:25-26 . . . .God is angry with the Israelites
for having other gods, so He
stirs up the Assyrian king
against the Israelites.

1 Chronicles 10:2-6 . . . . .King Saul, the first king of
Israel, when injured in battle
commits suicide along with his
armor bearer.

1 Chronicles 10:13-14 . . .King Saul is unfaithful to God,
so the Lord put him to death and

turns the kingdom over to David.

1 Chronicles 21:8-16 . . . .God is displeased with David and sends an angel to destroy Jerusalem. The Lord sends a plague on Israel, and seventy thousand men of Israel fall dead. However, He stops because He is grieved over the calamity.

2 Chronicles 13:13-18 . . .God helps Judah defeat Israel, and the Israelites suffer five hundred thousand casualties.

2 Chronicles 21:12-19 . . .God punishes King Jehoram for his evil leadership by giving him a bowel disease. In the course of time his bowels came out and he dies in great pain.

2 Chronicles 24:23-25 . . .God punishes Judah and Jerusalem. The Lord helps their enemies (Arameans) to conquer Judah and Jerusalem.

Esther 7:9-10 . . . . .Wicked Haman is hanged on the gallows that he builds to hang godly Mordecai.

Psalm 79:1-4 . . . . .God allows the Babylonians to conquer Jerusalem and ransack the temple because of the Israelites' disobedience to God.

Ecclesiastes 8:11-13 . . . .When the sentence for a crime is not quickly carried out, the hearts of people are filled with schemes to do wrong.

away, the birds of the air and the beasts of the earth to devour and destroy.

Jeremiah 17:10 . . . . .The Lord will search the heart and examine the mind, to reward a man according to his conduct (see John 34:11).

Jeremiah 19:9 . . . . .God will make the people of Judah and Jerusalem eat the flesh of their sons and daughters during the siege imposed by their enemies.

Jeremiah 21:1-10 . . . . . . .The leaders of Judah ask Jeremiah to implore the Lord for His protection against the attacking Babylonians. God refuses. God promises that anyone who surrenders and goes outside the walls will not be killed, but taken captive. All others will be killed.

Jeremiah 27:6 . . . . .God gives King Nebuchadnezzar the power to conquer Judah.

Jeremiah 29:4-9 . . . . . . .God gives instructions to Jeremiah how the people of Jerusalem are to live and behave while in captivity in Babylon.

Jeremiah 30:11 . . . . .God promises the people of Israel and Judah that He will not completely destroy them, but He will discipline them with justice.

Ezekiel 9:3-8 . . . . .God commands the killing of
the wicked in Jerusalem—men,
women, children, and the aged.
The man in linen, an angel, put
a mark on the forehead of the
godly, and they are spared.

Ezekiel 29:8-16 . . . . .God reduces Egypt to a desolate
wasteland for forty years. He
will then gather the Egyptians
from the nations, and they will
be a lowly kingdom.

Ezekiel 30:10-12 . . . . . . .God uses Nebuchadnezzar to
destroy Egypt.

Nahum 3:7-12 . . . . .Wicked Nineveh lays in ruins
and her infants are killed.

Acts 5:1-10 . . . . .A man named Ananias and his
wife Sapphira sell some proper-
ty and lie to the Holy Spirit by
keeping some of the money that
belongs to the Lord. They fall
dead on the spot.

Acts 12:21-23 . . . . .Because King Herod does not
give praise to God, an angel of
the Lord immediately strikes
him down, and he is eaten by
worms and dies.

Jude 7 . . . . .Sodom and Gomorrah and the
surrounding towns give them-
selves up to sexual immorality
and perversion. They serve as an
example of those who suffer the
punishment of eternal fire.

Revelation 18:7-8 . . . . . .Give her (Babylon) as much torture and grief as the glory and luxury she gives herself.

Revelation 20:15 . . . . . . .If anyone's name is not found written in the book of life, he will be thrown into the lake of fire.

REPENTANCE

2 Chronicles 7:14 . . . . . .If any of God's people will humble themselves and pray and seek God's face and turn from their wicked ways, God will forgive their sin and heal their land.

Proverbs 28:13 . . . . . . .He who conceals his sins does not prosper, but whoever confesses and renounces them finds mercy.

Ezekiel 18:32 . . . . .The Lord takes no pleasure in the death of anyone. Repent and live.

Matthew 3:1-3 . . . . .John the Baptist preaches, "Repent, for the kingdom of heaven is near."

Matthew 3:8 . . . . .Produce fruit in keeping with repentance.

Matthew 4:17 . . . . .Jesus preaches, "Repent, for the kingdom of heaven is near."

Luke 13:3 . . . . .Jesus says, "Repent or perish."

Luke 15:7 . . . . .There is more rejoicing in heaven over one sinner who repents than over ninety-nine righteous persons who do not need to repent.

Luke 24:47 . . . . .Repentance and forgiveness of sins will be preached in His (Christ's) name to all nations.

Acts 3:19 . . . . .Repent and turn to God, so that your sins may be wiped out, that times of refreshing may come from the Lord.

Acts 17:30 . . . . .In the past God overlooked ignorance, but now He commands all people everywhere to repent.

Romans 2:4 . . . . .God's kindness leads you to repentance.

2 Corinthians 7:10 . . . . . .Godly sorrow brings repentance that leads to salvation and leaves no regret, but worldly sorrow brings death.

2 Peter 3:9 . . . . .God doesn't want anyone to perish but everyone to come to repentance.

RESURRECTION

Job 19:25-26 . . . . .Job knows that after his skin has been destroyed, in his flesh he will see God.

Psalm 16:9-10 . . . . .King David writes that God will not abandon him to the grave or let God's Holy One see decay.

Psalm 49:15 . . . . .King David writes that God will redeem his soul from the grave.

Isaiah 26:19 . . . . .The dead will live. Their bodies will rise.

Ezekiel 37:1-14 . . . . .The Lord takes Ezekiel by the Spirit of the Lord to the middle of a valley full of dry bones. God puts flesh on the bones and tendons and breathes life into them—a vast army. The bones represent the whole house of Israel.

Daniel 12:2, 3 . . . . .The multitudes who sleep in the dust of the earth will awake, some to everlasting life and others to shame and everlasting contempt.

Matthew 16:21 . . . . .Jesus foretells His death and resurrection on the third day.

Matthew 27:52 . . . . .After Jesus' death the tombs open and the bodies of   many holy people who have died are raised to life. They come out of the tombs, and after Jesus' resurrection they go into the holy city (Jerusalem) and appear to many people.

Matthew 28:2-4 . . . . .An angel of the Lord comes down from heaven and rolls back the stone of the tomb and sits on it. His appearance is like lightning and his clothes are

white as snow. The guards shake
and become like dead men.

Matthew 28:5-10 . . . . . . .The angel tells Mary Magdalene
and the other Mary that Jesus
who is crucified has risen. They
meet Jesus on the way to Galilee
and clasp His feet and worship
him.

Mark 5:35-42 . . . . .Jesus brings a little girl back to
life.

Mark 8:31; 9:31 . . . . . . .Jesus tells His disciples about
His upcoming death and resur-
rection three days later.

Mark 12:25 . . . . .When the dead rise, they will
neither marry nor be given in
marriage. There will be no marriage in heaven. People will be
like angels in heaven.

Mark 16:2-7 . . . . .Mary Magdalene, Mary the
mother of James and Salome see
the stone of the tomb rolled
away. As they enter the tomb,
they see a young man dressed in
a white robe sitting on the right
side who says, "Jesus the
Nazarene, who is crucified, has
risen."

Luke 24:2-6 . . . . .The women find the stone of the
tomb rolled away. Suddenly two
men in clothes that gleam like
lightning stand beside them. The

men say that Jesus is not there.
He has risen .

ly body. If there is a natural body, there is also a spiritual body. Flesh and blood cannot inherit the kingdom of God.

Ephesians 4:9 . . . . .Christ descends to the lower earthly regions (hell).

1 Thessalonians 4:13-16 . . .The Lord Himself will come down from heaven with a loud command, with the voice of the archangel and the trumpet call of God, and the dead in Christ will rise first.

1 Thessalonians 4:17-18 . . .After that (verses 13-16) we who are still alive and are left will be caught up with the Lord in the clouds to meet the Lord in the air. And so we shall be with the Lord forever.

1 Peter 1:3 . . . . .In God's great mercy He gives us new birth into a living hope through the resurrection of Jesus Christ from the dead.

1 Peter 3:19-22 . . . . .While Jesus is in the tomb He preaches to the spirits in hell.

Revelation 1:5 . . . . .Jesus is the firstborn from the dead and ruler of the kings of the earth.

RULES, GOD'S

Genesis 3:16 . . . . .God increases woman's child-bearing pains. The woman's husband will rule over her.

Genesis 9:8-16 . . . . .God makes a covenant with Noah and man. The rainbow is set in the clouds. It will be a sign of the covenant between God and the earth. There will be no more floodwaters to destroy all life.

Exodus 20:3-17 . . . . .The Ten Commandments: You shall not have any other gods before me. You shall have no idols (make no graven images). You shall not misuse the Lord's name. Remember the Sabbath. Honor your mother and father. You shall not murder. You shall not commit adultery. You shall not steal. You shall not give false testimony. You shall not covet your neighbor's house (see Deuteronomy 5:6-21; Mark 10:19; Luke 18:20).

Genesis 35:4 . . . . .God has Jacob's household get rid of their foreign gods and rings in their ears. Jacob buries them under an oak at Shecham.

Leviticus 19:1-37 . . . . . . .The Lord gives Moses various laws regarding stealing, deceiving, fraud, hate, tattoos, etc.

Leviticus 19:28 . . . . .Do not put tattoo marks on yourselves.

Numbers 15:37-41 . . . . . .The Lord instructs the Israelites to make tassels for the corner of their garments as a reminder of God's commands.

Deuteronomy 8:11-14 . . .God warns the Israelites not to become proud because they have wealth and live in fine houses.

Deuteronomy 18:9-14 . . .God warns the Israelites against detestable practices such as sorcery, witchcraft, fortune telling, and witchcraft.

Deuteronomy 19:15 . . . . .One witness is not enough to convict a man accused of any crime. Two or more witnesses are required.

Deuteronomy 19:16-21 . .If a person is a false witness, show him no pity. It shall be life for life. eye for eye, tooth for tooth, hand for hand, foot for foot.

Deuteronomy 22:5 . . . . . .Women must not wear men's clothing, nor a man wear women's clothing.

Deuteronomy 23:23 . . . . .Whatever your lips utter, you must be sure to do.

Deuteronomy 23:24-25 . .You may eat all you want from your neighbor's field, but you must not put any into a basket.

Deuteronomy 25:1-3 . . . . .A guilty person is not to be
flogged more than forty lashes.

Deuteronomy 25:13-15 . .Do not have two different
weights in your bag. You must
have accurate and honest
weights and measures.

1 Chronicles 24:5 . . . . . .In the casting of lots, God
decides the outcome.

Psalm 32:8-11 . . . . .God will instruct us in the way
we should go.

Psalm 49:13-20 . . . . . . .People who prosper and trust in
themselves will after death never
see the light of life. A man who
has riches without understanding
is like the beasts that perish.

Psalm 53:2-3 . . . . .God looks down from heaven
and sees that no one is good, not
one.

Proverbs 6:16-19 . . . . . .Detestable things to the Lord are
haughty eyes, a lying tongue,
hands that shed innocent blood,
a heart that devises wicked
schemes, feet that rush into evil,
a false witness who pours out
lies, and a man who stirs up dis-
sension among brothers.

Proverbs 22:6 . . . . .Train a child in the way he
should go, and when he is old he
will not turn from it.

Isaiah 26:2-9 . . . . .God protects the righteous
nation who keeps faith with
Him.

Ezekiel 18:19-20 . . . . . . .A man's son will not be punished for the sins of the father,
nor the father punished for the
sins of his children. The person
who sins is the one who will die.

Ezekiel 18:21-22 . . . . . . .If a wicked man turns away
from all the sins he has commit-
ted and keeps all of God's
decrees, then none of the offenses he has committed will be
remembered.

Ezekiel 18:24 . . . . .If a righteous man turns from
his righteousness and commits
sin and does detestable things,
then none of the righteous things
he has done will be remembered

1Corinthians 11:14-15 . . .It is a disgrace for a man to have
long hair, but if a woman has
long hair, it is her glory.

2 Thessalonians 3:10 . . . .If a man will not work, he shall
not eat.

1 Timothy 3:6 . . . . .A church leader must not be a
recent convert, or he may
become conceited and fall under
the same judgment as the devil.

James 2:8 . . . . .Keep the royal law, which is,
"Love your neighbor as yourself."

SABBATH

Colossians 2:16 . . . . .Do not let anyone judge you by what you eat or drink or with regard to a religious festival, a new moon celebration, or a Sabbath day.

SACRIFICES

Genesis 22:2 . . . . .God tests Abraham by telling him to take his only son Isaac to the region of Moriah to offer him as a burnt offering. God then prevents Abraham from completing his sacrifice. (See Genesis 22:12).

Leviticus 18:21 . . . . .God forbids human sacrifices.

Psalm 106:37-38 . . . . . . .Pagans sacrifice their sons and daughters to demons.

John 15:13 . . . . .Greater love has no one than to lay down his own life for his friends.

Romans 12:1-2 . . . . .Offer your bodies as living sacrifices, holy and pleasing to God.

Hebrews 10:1-18 . . . . . . .Christ's sacrifice once for all.

Hebrews 11:32-40 . . . . . .Godly prophets and people suffer for God. God plans something better for them.

1 Peter 4:1-6 . . . . .Suffer for Christ. When your body suffers for Him, sin will lose its power.

1 John 2:2 . . . . .Jesus is the atoning sacrifice for
our sins, and not only for ours
but also for those of the whole
world.

SALVATION

Exodus 15:2 . . . . .The Lord is my strength, and He
has become my salvation.

Psalm 18:2 . . . . .The Lord is my rock, my
fortress, and my deliverer. He's
the horn of my salvation and my
stronghold.

Psalm 37:39 . . . . .The salvation of the righteous
comes from the Lord. He is their
stronghold in time of trouble.

Isaiah 12:2 . . . . .God is my salvation. Trust and
do not be afraid.

Isaiah 51:6 . . . . .God's salvation will last forever.

Jeremiah 15:19-21 . . . . . .God will save those who repent
and change their ways that they
may serve God.

Joel 2:32 . . . . .Everyone who calls on the name
of the Lord will be saved.

Matthew 6:33 . . . . .First, seek the Kingdom of God
and his righteousness, and all
these things will be given to you
as well.

Matthew 7:7 . . . . .Ask and it will be given. Seek
and you will find. Knock and
the door will be opened to you.

Matthew 10:32 . . . . .Acknowledge Jesus before men and He will acknowledge you before God.

Matthew 10:33 . . . . .Whoever disowns Jesus before men will be disowned before God.

Matthew 12:30 . . . . .Anyone not for Jesus is against Him.

Mark 8:38 . . . . .If we are ashamed of Jesus, He will also be ashamed of us.

Mark 13:13 . . . . .All men will hate you because of Christ, but he who stands firm to the end will be saved.

Mark 16:16 . . . . .He that believes (accepts Jesus Christ) and is baptized will be saved, and he who does not believe will be condemned.

Luke 12:4-5 . . . . .Do not fear those who can only kill the body, but fear him who after killing the body has power to throw you into hell.

Luke 12:8 . . . . .Whoever acknowledges Jesus before men will be acknowledged before the angels of God.

Luke 12:9 . . . . .Whoever disowns Jesus before men will be disowned before the angels of God.

John 1:12 . . . . .To all who receive Jesus and believe in His name He gives the right to become children of God.

John 2:19-21 . . . . Jesus says, "Destroy this temple,
and I will raise it again in three
days." The temple He speaks of
is His body.

John 3:3 . . . . Jesus declares that unless a man
is born again, he cannot enter
the kingdom of God.

John 3:14 . . . . Jesus predicts His being lifted
up on a cross.

John 3:15 . . . . Everyone who believes in Jesus
will have eternal life.

John 3:16 . . . . God so loved the world that He
gave his one and only Son, that
whoever believes in Him shall
not perish but have eternal life.

John 3:18 . . . . Whoever does not believe in
Jesus, God's one and only Son,
stands condemned.

John 3:36 . . . . Whoever believes in the Son
(Jesus) has eternal life, but who-
ever rejects the Son will not see
life, for God's wrath remains on
him.

John 5:21 . . . . The Father raises from the dead
and gives life. The Son (Jesus)
gives life to whom He is pleased
to give it.

John 5:22 . . . . God judges no one, but entrusts
all judgment to the Son (Jesus).

John 5:23 . . . . .He who does not honor Jesus
does not honor God who sent
him.

John 5:24 . . . . .Whoever hears Jesus' word and
believes in God will have eternal
life and not be condemned.

John 5:39-40 . . . . .Men study the Scriptures but
refuse to come to the Lord to
have eternal life.

John 11:25-26 . . . . .He who believes in Jesus will
live and never die (spiritually).

John 14:6 . . . . .No one comes to the Father
except through Jesus.

John 20:31 . . . . .Believing that Jesus is the
Christ, the Son of God, you may
have life in his name.

Acts 2:21 . . . . .Everyone who calls on the name
of the Lord will be saved.

Acts 4:10 . . . . .God raises Jesus from the dead,
and this man (Jesus) stands
before you completely healed.

Acts 4:12 . . . . .Salvation is found in no one else
but Jesus.

Acts 15:10-11 . . . . .We are saved through the grace
of our Lord Jesus.

Acts 16:30-31 . . . . .What must I do to be saved?
Believe in the Lord Jesus and be
saved.

Romans 1:16-17 . . . . . . .Apostle Paul's statement to the
Romans about God's plan of
salvation.

Romans 3:21-26 . . . . . . .Apostle Paul's description of
God's plan of salvation. For all
have sinned and fall short of the
glory of God. We are justified
by Christ's grace. We are
redeemed by believing and
accepting Jesus as our Savior.

Romans 5:8-11 . . . . .While we are still sinners, Christ
died for us.

Romans 6:23 . . . . .The wages of sin is death, but
the gift of God is eternal life in
Christ Jesus our Lord.

Romans 8:1-4, 13 . . . . . .There is now no judgment or
condemnation for those who are
in Christ Jesus, because through
Christ Jesus the law of the Spirit
of Life set us free from the law
of sin and death.

Romans 9:30-33 . . . . . . .We are saved by faith, not by
good works.

Romans 10:9-10, 13 . . . .If you confess with your mouth,
"Jesus is Lord," and believe in
your *heart* that God raised Him
from the dead, you will be
saved. Everyone who calls upon
the name of the Lord will be
saved.

Romans 11:5-6 . . . . .At the present time there is a
remnant chosen by grace. And if

by grace, then it is no longer by works. If it were, grace would no longer be grace.

Romans 11:11 . . . . .Salvation has come to the Gentiles to make Israel envious.

1Corinthians 2:13-14 . . . .Worldly people cannot under-stand God's plan. The Holy Spirit is not in them.

2 Corinthians 5:17 . . . . . .Christians are a new creation.

2 Corinthians 7:10-11 . . .Godly sorrow brings repentance that leads to salvation. But worldly sorrow brings death.

Galatians 2:21 . . . . .Righteousness cannot be gained through the law, only by grace.

Galatians 3:26-29 . . . . . .Salvation is for everyone who has faith in Christ Jesus.

Ephesians 1.4-5 . . . . .God chooses us before the cre-ation of the world (See Romans 8:28-30).

Ephesians 2:5, 8-9 . . . . . .We are saved by grace, through faith, and this not from your-selves. It is the gift of God, not by works, so that no one can boast .

Colossians 1:22-23 . . . . .We are   reconciled by Christ's physical body through death to present you holy in God's sight.

1 Thessalonians 5:9 . . . . .God did not appoint us to suffer wrath but to receive salvation through our Lord Jesus Christ.

2 Thessalonians 2:13-14 . . .God chooses us (believers) from the beginning.

1 Timothy 1:15-17 . . . . . .The apostle Paul claims that he is the worst sinner, yet he is saved.

1 Timothy 2:4-5 . . . . .God wants everyone to be saved.

2 Timothy 1:9-10 . . . . . .We are saved by grace.

Hebrews 1:14 . . . . .People who will inherit salvation have guardian angels (ministering spirits).

Hebrews 5:8-10 . . . . . . .Jesus becomes the source of eternal salvation for all who obey him.

Hebrews 7:24-25 . . . . . . .Jesus saves completely.

Hebrews 10:14 . . . . . . .Christ's sacrifice made us (believers) perfect in God's eyes.

Hebrews 10:39 . . . . .Those who shrink back are destroyed. Those who believe are saved.

1 Peter 1:7-9 . . . . .Believing in Jesus Christ gives us glorious joy, for we are receiving the goal of our faith— the salvation of our souls.

1 Peter 3:18-22 . . . . . . .Jesus is put to death, but made alive by the spirit.

1 John 2:22-23 . . . . .If you deny Christ, you deny God.

1 John 4:2 . . . . .To recognize the spirit of God, you must believe that Jesus Christ has come in the flesh.

Failure to acknowledge this is not from God, but from the antichrist.

1 John 5:10-13 . . . . .God has given us eternal life through His Son. He who has the Son has life. He who does not have the Son does not have life.

Revelation 1:18 . . . . .Jesus holds the keys to death and hades (hell).

Revelation 2:11 . . . . .He who overcomes will not be hurt by the second death (hell).

Revelation 3:15-16 . . . . .The church in Laodicea is warned that if they are lukewarm (for Jesus) He will spit them out of His mouth.

SANCTITY OF LIFE (SEE ABORTION)

SATAN

Genesis 3:1-6 . . . . .Satan tempts and lies to Eve in the Garden of Eden when she eats the forbidden fruit. She gives some to Adam.

Job 1:6-12 . . . . .God allows Satan to test Job.

Isaiah 14:12-15 . . . . . . .Satan falls from heaven and is cast down to earth.

Ezekiel 28:14-19 . . . . . .Satan is a guardian cherub who is expelled and thrown to earth.

Matthew 4:1-4 . . . . .Satan tempts Jesus.

John 8:42-47 . . . . .Believe in God, not Satan who is a murderer and the father of liars.

John 14:30 . . . . .The prince of this world (Satan) has no power over Jesus.

2 Corinthians 11:13-15 . . .Satan masquerades as an angel of light and his servants as apostles of Christ .

Ephesians 2:1-3 . . . . .Satan is the ruler of the kingdom of the air, and it is his spirit at work in those who are disobedient.

Ephesians 6:10-11 . . . . . .Be strong in the Lord and put on the full armor of God to be able to stand against the devil.

Ephesians 6:12 . . . . .Our struggle is not against people but against the powers of the dark world and spiritual forces of evil in the heavenly realms.

2 Thessalonians 2:3-4 . . .Do not let Satan deceive you.

2 Thessalonians 2:8 . . . . .The Lord will overthrow and destroy Satan with the breath of His mouth.

2 Thessalonians 2:9 . . . . .Be watchful of Satan's counterfeit miracles, signs, and wonders.

2 Thessalonians 2:10 . . . .Men perish because they refuse to love the truth and to be saved. Satan works to get men to love anything but the truth and so be saved.

James 3:13-16 . . . . .Envy and selfish ambition are from Satan.

James 4:7 . . . . .Submit to God. Resist the devil, and he will flee from you.

1 Peter 5:8 . . . . .Be self-controlled and alert. The devil prowls around like a roaring lion looking for someone to devour.

Revelation 12:7-9 . . . . . .Michael and his angels fight with Satan and throws Satan down to earth.

Revelation 13:8 . . . . .All inhabitants of the earth whose names are not written in the book of life will worship the beast (Satan).

Revelation 13:11-15 . . . .Satan performs miracles on earth, including causing fire to come down from the sky to earth in full view of men.

Revelation 13:16-18 . . . .Satan will force unbelievers to receive the mark of the beast on their right hands or foreheads. The number of the beast is 666.

Revelation 14:9-11 . . . . .Anyone who worships the beast (Satan) and receives his mark on the forehead or hand will feel God's wrath and be tormented with burning sulfur forever and ever. *Do not accept the mark of the beast.*

Revelation 19:20 . . . . . . .Satan and the false prophet will
be thrown into the fiery lake of
burning sulfur.

Revelation 20:1-3 . . . . . .Satan will be thrown into the
abyss (hell) for a thousand
years.

Revelation 20:10 . . . . . . .The devil will be thrown into the
lake of fire of burning sulfur
(hell) where he and the false
prophet will be tormented day
and night forever and ever.

SECOND COMING OF CHRIST

Isaiah 26:21 . . . . .The Lord is coming out of his
dwelling to punish the people of
the earth for their sins (See
Isaiah 66:15-16).

Daniel 7:13-14 . . . . .Daniel has a vision where he
sees one like a son of man
(Christ) coming with the clouds
of heaven.

Matthew 16:27 . . . . . . .The Son of man is coming in
God's glory with His angels and
He will reward each person
according to what he has done.

Matthew 24:3-13 . . . . . . .The disciples ask when the Lord
will come, and Jesus tells them
what to look for.

Matthew 24:14 . . . . .Jesus states that the gospel will
be preached to all the world,
then He will return.

Matthew 24:23-27 . . . . . .False reporting of Christ's
return.

Matthew 24:30-31 . . . . . .The Son of Man (Jesus) will be
coming in the clouds of the sky.
He will send His angels with a
loud trumpet call to gather His
elect (believers) from one end of
the heavens to the other.

Matthew 24:36 . . . . .No one knows the day or hour
of Christ's return, not even the
angels in heaven, nor the Son,
but only the Father.

Mark 13:32-37 . . . . .No one knows the time of
Christ's return.

Luke 12:40 . . . . .Christ will return when we do
not expect Him.

Luke 21:25-26 . . . . .Men will faint from terror,
apprehensive of what is coming
on the world. The heavenly bodies will be shaken.

Luke 21:27-28 . . . . .The Son of Man (Jesus) will be
coming in a cloud with power
and great glory. Your redemption
is drawing near.

Acts 1:10-11 . . . . .Suddenly two men dressed in
white stand beside the apostles.
"Men of Galilee," they say,
"why do you stand here looking
into the sky? This same Jesus,
who is taken from you into
heaven, will come back in the

same way you have seen him go into heaven.

1 Corinthians 15:50-58 . .Flesh and blood cannot inherit the kingdom of God. At the last trumpet we will be changed in a flash—in the twinkling of an eye.

1 Thessalonians 4:13-14 . . .God will bring with Jesus those who have fallen asleep in Him (the dead in Christ).

1 Thessalonians 4:16 . . . .The Lord Himself will come down from heaven, with a loud command, with the voice of the archangel and the trumpet call of God, and the dead in Christ will rise first.

1 Thessalonians 4:17 . . . .Then those who are still alive and are left will be caught up with them in the clouds to meet the Lord in the air, and so we will be with the Lord forever.

1 Thessalonians 5:23-24 . . .Keep holy until Christ returns.

2 Thessalonians 1:6-10 . .Jesus will punish the unbelievers with everlasting destruction when He returns.

2 Thessalonians 2:5-12 . .The coming of the lawless one (antichrist) will be revealed. God's restrainer is holding him back, but Jesus will overthrow him with the breath of His mouth.

Hebrews 9:27 . . . . .Man dies once and after that he faces judgment.

Hebrews 9:28 . . . . .Christ is sacrificed once to take away the sins of many people. He will appear a second time, not to bear sin, but bring salvation to those who are waiting for Him.

2 Peter 3:10-13 . . . . . . .Christ will come like a thief and everything will be destroyed. You ought to live holy and godly lives.

Revelation 1:7 . . . . .Everyone will see Jesus when He comes.

Revelation 3:10-11 . . . . .Hold on to what you have (faith). I am coming. Jesus will keep you from the hour of trial that is going to come upon the whole world to test those who live on earth.

Revelation 3:12 . . . . .The name of the city of my God, the new Jerusalem, is coming down out of heaven from my God.

Revelation 14:15-20 . . . .The angels will harvest the earth, throwing the wicked into the winepress of God's wrath.

Revelation 20:4-6 . . . . . .The first resurrection is a one-thousand-year reign. The second death (spiritual) will have no power over the blessed and holy (believers).

Revelation 21:8 . . . . .The ungodly will all take their place in the fiery lake of burning sulfur. This is the second death.

SECURITY OF SALVATION

Psalm 13:5 . . . . .David trusts in God's unfailing love and rejoices in his salvation.

Psalm 17:15 . . . . .David expects to see God when he awakes from death.

Psalm 23:1-6 . . . . .The Lord is my shepherd. I shall lack nothing.

Matthew 28:20 . . . . .Jesus will be with believers always, to the very end of the age.

John 10:27-30 . . . . .The Lord's sheep (believers) are given eternal life. They shall never perish. No one can snatch them out of God's hand. Jesus and God are one.

John 17:12 . . . . .Believers are kept safe through Jesus.

Romans 8:35-39 . . . . . . .Nothing can separate us (believers) from the love of God that is in Christ Jesus.

Romans 11:29 . . . . .God's gifts and His call (salvation) are irrevocable.

Ephesians 1:13-14 . . . . . .Believing in Christ guarantees our godly inheritance.

Philippians 1:6 . . . . .Christ's good work in you will
continue to completion until the
day of Christ Jesus.

2 Timothy 4:18 . . . . .The Lord will rescue us (believers) from every evil attack and
bring us safely to His heavenly
Kingdom.

1 Peter 1:3-5 . . . . .Our inheritance through Christ
can never perish, spoil or fade.
Believers are shielded.

1 John 5:11-13 . . . . .He who has the Son (Christ) has
life. He who does not have the
Son of God does not have life.
God has given us eternal life,
and this life is in his Son
(Jesus).

Revelation 3:5 . . . . .He who overcomes will never
have his name erased from the
book of life.

SEXUAL SINS

Genesis 19:30-38 . . . . . . .ot's daughters make their father
drunk with wine. They sleep
with him without his knowledge,
and they become pregnant.

Exodus 22:19 . . . . .Anyone who has sexual relations
with an animal must be put to
death.

Leviticus 18:1-30 . . . . . . .The Lord gives Moses a list of
unlawful sexual relationships
(see Leviticus 20:10-21)

Deuteronomy 22:22 . . . . .If a man sleeps with another
                            man's wife, both must die.

Deuteronomy 22:25 . . . . .If a man rapes a girl who is
                            pledged to be married, only the
                            man must die.

Judges 16:1 . . . . .Samson spends one night with a
                            prostitute.

2 Samuel 11:2-5 . . . . . . .King David sleeps with
                            Bathsheba, who is married. She
                            becomes pregnant.

Proverbs 5:1-6 . . . . .Avoid adultery.

Proverbs 7:10-27 . . . . . .Be attentive against the ways of
                            a prostitute.

Matthew 5:27-28 . . . . . .Anyone who looks at a woman
                            lustfully has already committed
                            adultery with her in his heart.

Romans 1:26-27 . . . . . .God gave people over to their
                            shameful lusts. Men and women
                            exchange natural relations for
                            unnatural ones (homosexual).

1 Corinthians 5:11 . . . . .Do not associate with a
                            Christian who indulges in sexual
                            sins, greed, swindling, etc.

1 Corinthians 6:13-20 . . .The body is not meant for sexual
                            immorality. Your body is a tem-
                            ple of the Holy Spirit. Therefore,
                            honor God with your body.

1 Corinthians 10:8-10 . . .Do not commit sexual immorali-
                            ty as some have done in Israel's
                            past. In one day twenty- three

                          thousand of them die. Do not
                          test the Lord.

Galatians 5:19-21 . . . . . .The acts of the sinful nature are:
                          sexual immorality, impurity and
                          debauchery, etc. Those who live
                          like this will not inherit the
                          kingdom of God.

Ephesians 5:3 . . . . .There must not even be a hint of
                          sexual immorality, any kind of
                          impurity, or of greed with God's
                          people.

Colossians 3:5 . . . . .Put to death whatever belongs
                          to your earthly nature: sex-
                          ual immorality, impurity,
                          lust,   evil desires, and
                          greed, which is idolatry.

1 Thessalonians 4:3-8 . . .Avoid sexual immorality. Learn
                          to control your own body.

SINS

Genesis 3:6-19 . . . . .Adam and Eve commit the first
                          sin by eating from the tree of
                          knowledge of good and evil in
                          the middle of the Garden of
                          Eden. This causes death to come
                          to the world.

Exodus 23:1-3 . . . . .Do not help a wicked man by
                          being a malicious witness. Do
                          not follow the crowd in doing
                          wrong.

Exodus 23:8 . . . . .Do not accept a bribe, for a
bribe blinds those who see and
twists the words of the righteous.

Leviticus 16:6-10 . . . . . . .This story is the explanation of
the term *scapegoat* (the goat that
did not get killed) used for
Aaron's sin atonement.

Deuteronomy 28:53-57 . .Cannibalism is predicted in
Israel—that the Hebrews will
come under siege and become so
desperate they will eat the flesh
of their sons and daughters.
They will not share the human
flesh. Women will eat their own
children after they are born.

2 Kings 14:6 . . . . .Everyone must pay for his own
sins. Fathers shall not be put to
death for their children, nor
children put to death for their
fathers.

1 Chronicles 10:13-14 . . .King Saul, the first king of
Israel, dies because he is
unfaithful to the Lord. He did
not keep the word of the Lord,
he consults with a witch for
guidance, and he does not
inquire of the Lord.

2 Chronicles 6:36 . . . . . .All have sinned.

Job 13:28 . . . . .Man wastes away like something rotten.

Ezekiel 18:21 . . . . .If a wicked man turns away from all the sins he has committed and keeps all the decrees of God, he will surely live—he will not spiritually die. None of the offenses he has committed will be remembered against him.

Amos 1:13 . . . . .Ammon rips open the pregnant women of Gilead.

Matthew 1:21 . . . . .Jesus will save his people (believers) from their sins.

Matthew 15:19 . . . . .Man's heart is the source of sin.

Matthew 18:6 . . . . .If anyone causes a little child who believes in Jesus to sin, that person will be severely punished.

Matthew 18:15-17 . . . . . .If a Christian brother sins against you, go and show him his faults just between the two of you, but if he will not listen, secure the testimony of two or three witnesses.

Mark 3:29 . . . . .Whoever blasphemes the Holy Spirit will never be forgiven. He is guilty of an eternal sin.

Luke 5:24 . . . . .The Son of Man (Christ Jesus) has authority on earth to forgive sins.

Luke 16:8 . . . . .The worldly are shrewder in dealing with their own kind than

are the people of the light
(Christians).

Luke 17:1 . . . . .Jesus says, "Things that cause
people to sin are bound to come,
but woe to that person through
whom they come."

John 8:7 . . . . .Jesus says, "If anyone is without
sin, let him be the first to throw
a stone."

Romans 3:10 . . . . .There is no one righteous, not
even one.

Romans 3:23 . . . . .All have sinned and fall short of
the glory of God.

Romans 6:23 . . . . .The wages of sin is death, but
the gift of God is eternal life in
Christ Jesus our Lord.

Galatians 5:19-26 . . . . . .The acts of the sinful nature will
not lead to the kingdom of God.

Galatians 6:1 . . . . .Gently restore people who are
caught up in sin, but be careful
not to be tempted.

1 Timothy 5:20 . . . . . . .Publicly rebuke those who sin,
so that others may take warning.

Hebrews 12:6 . . . . .The Lord disciplines those He
loves, and He punishes everyone
He accepts as a son.

James 1:13 . . . . .God cannot be tempted by evil,
nor does he tempt anyone.

James 1:21 . . . . .Get rid of all moral filth and the evil that is so prevalent, and humbly accept the Word planted in you, which can save you.

1 Peter 4:8 . . . . .Love each other deeply, because love covers a multitude of sins.

1 John 1:7 . . . . .If believers walk in the light with Christ Jesus, He will purify us from every sin.

1 John 1:8 . . . . .If we claim to be without sin, we deceive ourselves and the truth is not in us.

1 John 1:9 . . . . .If believers confess their sins, He is faithful and just and will forgive their sins and purify them from all unrighteousness.

1 John 1:10 . . . . .If we claim we have not sinned, we make Him out to be a liar, and His word has no place in our lives.

SODOM AND GOMORRAH

Genesis 18:20 . . . . .The Lord says, "The outcry against Sodom and Gomorrah is so great and the sin so grievous that I will go down to see it for myself."

Genesis 19:4-5 . . . . .The men from Sodom call to Lot. They want sex with the strangers (angels) who are visiting Lot.

Genesis 19:10-12 . . . . . . .The strangers (angels) visiting
Lot strike the men at Lot's door
with blindness (see Genesis
19:4-5).

Genesis 19:13-25 . . . . . . .God destroys Sodom and
Gomorrah and all the plains and
vegetation by raining down
burning sulfur. But He spares
Lot and his family.

Genesis 19:26-29 . . . . . . .The angels instruct Lot and his
family not to look back, but
Lot's wife does, and she
becomes a pillar of salt (verse
26).

Genesis 19:30-38 . . . . . . .Lot's daughters get their father
drunk with wine. They sleep
with him without his knowledge
and they become pregnant.

Deuteronomy 29:23 . . . . .The cities of Admah and
Zeboiim are destroyed like
Sodom and Gomorrah.

Jeremiah 50:40 . . . . .God also destroys the neighbor-
ing cities of Sodom and
Gomorrah.

Ezekiel 16:49-50 . . . . . . .Sodom's sins are arrogance,
gluttony, and lack of concern.
They do not help the poor and
needy. They are haughty and do
detestable things before God.

Ezekiel 16:53 . . . . .God will restore Sodom.

Jude 7 . . . . .Sodom and Gomorrah and the
surrounding towns give them-
selves up to sexual immorality
and perversion and will suffer
the punishment of eternal fire.

Spiritual Gifts

Romans 12:6-8 . . . . . . .Spiritual gifts of: *prophecy* (also
1 Corinthians 12:10, 28;
Ephesians 4:11), *service* (also
Acts 6:1-6), *teaching* (also 1
Corinthians 12:28; Ephesians
4:11), *exhortation* (encourage
and comfort), *giving* (also Luke
21:1-4; 2 Corinthians 8:1-5;
Philippians 4:15-19), *leadership*
(also Acts 20:17-38), and *mercy*.

1 Corinthians 7:7-9 . . . . .Spiritual gift of *celibacy* (also 1
Corinthians 7:25-40).

1 Corinthians 12:8 . . . . . .Spiritual gifts of *wisdom* (also
Acts 6:10) and *knowledge*.

1 Corinthians 12:9 . . . . . .Spiritual gifts of *faith* and *heal-
ing* (also Acts 9:32-35;   1
Corinthians 12:28).

1 Corinthians12:10, 28 . .Spiritual gifts of *miracles*, *dis-
cernment* (also Acts 5:1-11;
8:18-23), *speaking in tongues*
(also 1 Corinthians 12:30; 14:5-
13), *interpretation of tongues*
(also 1 Corinthians 14:5-13).

1 Corinthians 12:28-29 . . .Spiritual gifts of *apostles* (also Ephesians 4:11), *helps* (also Romans 16:1-2), *administration*.

Ephesians 4:11 . . . . .Spiritual gifts of *evangelist*. and *pastor*.

1 Peter 4:9-10 . . . . .Spiritual gift of *hospitality*.

SUCCESS

Genesis 39:3 . . . . .The Lord gives Joseph success.

Deuteronomy 8:11-14 . . .When you are living well, be careful not to become proud and forget the Lord.

Deuteronomy 28:2-6 . . . .You will be blessed if you obey the Lord.

Joshua 1:7-8 . . . . .The Lord instructs Joshua to meditate on the Book of the Law day and night so that he may be careful to do everything written in it. Then he will be prosperous and successful.

2 Chronicles 26:3-5 . . . . .King Uzziah is given success as long as he seeks the Lord.

Nehemiah 2:20 . . . . .The God of heaven gives success.

Psalm 25:12-13 . . . . .Fear the Lord and prosper.

Psalm 35:4-9 . . . . .King David asks for God's judgment for those who plan to harm him.

Psalm 37:5-13 . . . . .Commit to the Lord, and He will help you and punish the wicked. The meek will inherit the land.

Psalm 118:25 . . . . .King David asks God for success.

Proverbs 16:3 . . . . .Commit to the Lord whatever you do. Your plans will succeed.

Ecclesiastes 10:10 . . . . . .Skill will bring success.

Matthew 6:32 . . . . .Seek first God's kingdom and his righteousness, and all these things will follow.

SUFFERING

Job 1:1- 22 . . . . .The forty-two chapters of the book of Job depicts tremendous suffering.

Acts 14:22 . . . . .Christians must endure many hardships to enter the kingdom of God.

Romans 5:3-5 . . . . .The problems we face are good for us. They produce perseverance, character, and hope .

Romans 8:17 . . . . .Believers share in Christ's suffering in order that they may also share in his glory.

Romans 8:18 . . . . .Present suffering by believers are not worth comparing with the glory that will be reveled to us.

Romans 12:1-2 . . . . .Offer your body to God. Be not of this world.

Galatians 2:20 . . . . .We are crucified with Christ.

Galatians 6:2 . . . . .Carry each other's burdens.

Philippians 1:29 . . . . .It is granted to believers to suffer on behalf of Christ.

Philippians 4:11-13 . . . . .Be content whatever the circumstances.

1 Thessalonians 4:13 . . . .Do not grieve like the rest of the world when Christians die.

2 Timothy 2:12 . . . . .If we suffer, with Christ, we will also reign with Him.

2 Timothy 3:12 . . . . .Everyone who wants to live a godly life in Christ Jesus will be persecuted.

James 1:2-4 . . . . .Consider it pure joy whenever you face trials of many kinds, because the testing of your faith develops perseverance.

1 Peter 2:19 . . . . .It is commendable to suffer unjustly because you are conscious of God.

1 Peter 3:14 . . . . .But even if you should suffer for what is right, you will be blessed.

1 Peter 4:12-19 . . . . .Rejoice that you suffer for Christ.

1 Peter 5:8-9 . . . . .Stand firm in your faith, because Christians around the world are

undergoing the same kind of
suffering.

1 Peter 5:10 . . . . .After you have suffered a little
while for Christ, you will be
restored.

SUICIDE

1 Samuel 31:1-6 . . . . . . .King Saul, first king of Israel,
and his armor bearer commit sui-
cide (see I Chronicles 10:2-6).

2 Samuel 17:1 . . . . .Ahithophel hangs himself.

1 Kings 16:18 . . . . .Zimri, King of Israel, commits
suicide.

Matthew 27:5 . . . . .Judas Iscariot (who betrays
Jesus) throws the money he is
paid for betrayal into the temple
and then he hangs himself.

Acts 16:27-28 . . . . .The Philippian jailer is tempted
to commit suicide but apostle
Paul stops him.

TEMPLE

2 Samuel 7:12-13 . . . . . .David's son is to build the
temple

1 Kings 8:1-21 . . . . .The Ark of the Covenant is
brought to the temple (verse 6).

1 Chronicles 22:14 . . . . .King David and his son
Solomon build a temple to the
Lord using 3,750 tons of gold

         and 37,500 tons of silver, plus other materials.

2 Chronicles 3:1-17 . . . . .King Solomon builds the temple to the Lord.

2 Chronicles 12:9-12 . . . .Because of the sin of King Rehoboam, son of Solomon, King Shishak of Egypt attacks Israel and carries off the temple treasures.

Matthew 24:2 . . . . .Jesus predicts the temple destruction (see Mark 13:2).

John 2:14-16 . . . . .Jesus drives out the money-changers from the temple.

Revelation 21:22 . . . . . . .There are no temples in heaven. The Lord God Almighty and Jesus are its temple.

TEMPTATION

Psalm 39:1 . . . . .Put a muzzle on your mouth as long as the wicked are in your presence.

Matthew 4:1-11 . . . . . . .Satan tempts Jesus in the desert.

Mark 14:38 . . . . .Pray so that you will not fall into temptation. The spirit is willing but the body is weak.

Luke 4:12 . . . . .Do not test the Lord.

Romans 14:13 . . . . .Do not judge one another.

1 Corinthians 10:13 . . . . .No temptation has seized you except what is common to man. God will not let you be tempted

beyond what you can bear, but when you are tempted, He will provide a way out so that you can stand up under it.

1 Corinthians 15:33-34 . .Bad company corrupts good character.

2 Corinthians 6:14 . . . . . .Do not be yoked together with unbelievers.

Galatians 6:1 . . . . .Beware of temptation.

1 Timothy 6:7-10 . . . . . .For the love of money is a root of all kinds of evil. Be content with food and clothes, not riches.

2 Timothy 2:19 . . . . .Christians must turn away from wickedness.

Hebrews 4:15 . . . . .Jesus is tempted in every way, just as we are, yet He is without sin.

James 1:13 . . . . .God does not tempt anyone.

James 1:26-27 . . . . .Keep a tight rope on your tongues. Keep from being polluted by the world.

James 2:1-7 . . . . .Do not show favoritism.

James 5:12 . . . . .Do not swear, or God will call you to account.

2 Peter 2:20-22 . . . . . . .If a Christian escapes the corruption of the world and then is entangled in it, he will be worse off than if he had never been a believer.

1 John 2:15 . . . . .Do not love the world or anything in it.

1 John 2:16 . . . . .The cravings of sinful man, the
lust of his eyes, and the boasting
of what he has and does, comes
from the world, not the Father.
The man who does the will of
God lives forever (spiritually).

Revelation 3:2 . . . . .Wake up. Your deeds are not
complete in the sight of God.

TEN COMMANDMENTS

Exodus 20:3-17 . . . . .The Ten Commandments: You
shall have no other gods before
Me. You shall have no idols. You
shall not misuse the Lord's
name. Remember the Sabbath.
Honor your mother and father.
You shall not murder. You shall
not commit adultery. You shall
not steal. You shall not give false
testimony. You shall not covet
(see Deuteronomy 5:6-21; Mark
10:19; Luke 18:20).

Exodus 31:18 . . . . .Moses is given two tablets of
stone on which the Ten
Commandments are written.

Leviticus 19:11-31 . . . . . .God gives Moses various laws
by which to live.

Deuteronomy 5:29 . . . . . .The Lord wants us to keep all of
His commands always, so that it
might go well with us and our
children forever.

TESTING, GOD'S

Genesis 21:8-20 . . . . .Abraham sends Hagar (Sarah's slave) and her son, Ishmael, who is fathered by Abraham, away into the desert.

Genesis 22:1-18 . . . . .God instructs Abraham to sacrifice his son Isaac. At the last minute God spares Isaac.

Genesis 32:24-32 . . . . . .Jacob wrestles with God and is blessed. God wrenches Jacob's hip socket. His name is changed to Israel, which means, "He struggles with God."

Numbers 22:21-34 . . . . . .Balaam beats his donkey, and the donkey speaks to him. The Lord opens Balaam's eyes.

2 Chronicles 32:31 . . . . .God left Hezekiah to test him and know everything that was in his heart.

Job 1:6-12 . . . . .God and Satan have a discussion. God allows Satan to torment Job but not kill him.

Psalm 119:19 . . . . .God's people are strangers on earth.

Luke 4:12 . . . . .Jesus says, "Do not put the Lord your God to the test."

James 1:12 . . . . .Blessed is the man who perseveres under trial, because when he has stood the test, he will receive the crown of life.

TONGUES

TOOLS

1 Chronicles 20:3 . . . . . .King David conquers people to labor with saws, iron picks, and axes.

1 Chronicles 28:17 . . . . .Gold forks are used.

TRANSFIGURATION

Matthew 17:2-9 . . . . . . .Jesus is transfigured on a mountain before Peter, James, and John, the brother of James. Moses and Elijah appear with Jesus.

Mark 9:2-10 . . . . .Jesus is transfigured and appears with Elijah and Moses. His clothes become dazzling white—whiter than anyone in the world could bleach them.

Luke 9:28-36 . . . . .Peter, John, and James accompany Jesus to a mountain to pray. Jesus changes and becomes as bright as lightning. Two men—Moses and Elijah—appear with Him in glorious splendor. They speak of the coming crucifixion of Jesus.

2 Peter 1:16-18 . . . . .Peter, John, and James are eyewitnesses of Jesus' majesty on the sacred Mount of Transfiguration.

TRIBULATION PERIOD

Isaiah 24:1-6 . . . . .God will devastate the earth.

Daniel 7:1-14 . . . . .Daniel dreams about the end
times and God's judgment.

Daniel 7:15-28 . . . . .Daniel interprets the dream that
is about the end times and the
tribulation period.

Daniel 12:1-13 . . . . .The end times are described in
the book of Daniel.

Joel 2:30-32 . . . . .The Day of the Lord will be
dreadful for nonbelievers, the
sun will turn to darkness and the
moon to blood. Everyone who
calls on the name of the Lord
will be saved.

Zephaniah 1:2-3 . . . . . . .God's wrath will sweep away
everything at the end of the
world, as we know it.

Zechariah 14:12-13 . . . . .There will be a plague that God
will inflict on those who fight
against Jerusalem. Their flesh
will rot while they are standing
on their feet, their eyes will rot
in their sockets, and their
tongues will rot in their mouths.

Mark 13:20 . . . . .The tribulation will be so bad
that only for the sake of the elect
(believers) will God shorten the
days, or no one will
survive.

2 Thessalonians 2:4 . . . . .The antichrist will set himself
up in God's temple and proclaim
himself to be God.

Revelation 6:6 . . . . .When Jesus opens the third of
seven seals, the results on living
standards in the final days is
revealed—a quart of wheat or
three quarts of barley will sell
for one day's wages.

Revelation 9:1-11 . . . . . .Locusts that sting like scorpions
will torment the wicked in the
final days.

Revelation 9:18 . . . . .One-third of mankind will be
killed in the final days by the
three plagues of fire, smoke, and
sulfur.

Revelation 11:1-12 . . . . .The seven years tribulation
period divided into two
segments.

Revelation 14:9-13 . . . . .People who accept the mark of
the beast will taste God's fury.
*Do not accept the mark of the
beast.*

Revelation 16:2-4 . . . . . .People who accept the mark of
the beast will break out with
sores, the sea and rivers turn into
blood.

Revelation 16:21 . . . . . . .The final days will see one- hun-
dred-pound hailstones fall from
the sky.

TROUBLESOME PEOPLE

Job 5:7 . . . . .Man is born to trouble as surely
as sparks fly upward.

John 16:33 . . . . .In this world you will have trouble, but Jesus has overcome the
world.

Titus 1:15 . . . . .To the pure, all things are pure.
But to those who are corrupt,
nothing is pure—their minds
and consciences are corrupt.

Titus 3:9-11 . . . . .Warn a divisive person once or
twice. After that, have nothing to
do with him.

James 4:1-3 . . . . .The reason for quarrels is the
evil desires that dwell within us.

James 4:4 . . . . .Friendship with the world is
hatred toward God.

WILDERNESS WANDERING

Exodus 15:22-26 . . . . . . .God uses a piece of wood to
sweeten the drinking water at
Marah.

Exodus 16:10-36 . . . . . . .God provides manna from heav-
en for the Israelites in the desert
(manna is like white coriander
seed and tastes like wafers made
with honey). God also provides
quail to eat.

Exodus 17:1-7 . . . . .God provides water for the
Israelites by having Moses strike
a rock with his staff. Water
flows from the rock at Massah
and Meribah.

Exodus 17:10-13 . . . . . . .Moses and Joshua fight the
Amalekites. They defeat them as
long as Moses holds his hands up.

Exodus 20:22-26 . . . . . . .God instructs Moses to make an
altar for him and not to use
dressed stones or make any
other gods alongside of his altar.

Exodus 40:34-38 . . . . . . .The cloud (symbolizing God's
presence) covers the Tent of
Meeting and whenever it lifts,
the Israelites will move. The fire
is in the cloud at night.

Numbers 11:4-5 . . . . .The Israelites complain about
the food (manna).

Numbers 12:1-13 . . . . . . .Aaron and his sister Miriam
challenge Moses. God punishes
Miriam by giving her leprosy for
seven days.

Numbers 12:3 . . . . .Moses is the most humble man
on the face of the earth.

Numbers 14:26-35 . . . . . .The Israelites are not faithful to
the Lord, so He denies them
entry into the Promised Land for
forty years. Only Caleb and
Joshua will see the Promised
Land, because they remain
faithful.

Deuteronomy 9:1-4 . . . . .God goes before the Israelites into the Promised Land to destroy the nations across the Jordan River. He does this, not because of the Israelite's right-eousness but rather because of the wickedness of the pagan nations (see Genesis 17:7-8).

Deuteronomy 9:4-6 . . . . .God drives out the people of Canaan and gives the land over.

Deuteronomy 29:5-6 . . . .During the forty years in the desert, the clothes and sandals do not wear out. They do not eat bread, drink wine or other fer-mented drinks.

Joshua 5:11-12 . . . . .God stops the manna from heav-en the day after the Israelites eat the produce from the land of Canaan.

WINE

Genesis 9:20-21 . . . . .Noah plants a vineyard, drinks some of its wine, and becomes drunk.

Genesis 14:18 . . . . .Melchizedek king of Salem (Jerusalem) brings out bread and wine. He is priest of God, and he blesses Abram.

Genesis 27:28 . . . . .May God give you of heaven's dew and of earth's richness an abundance of grain and new wine.

Deuteronomy 14:25-26 . .God gives instructions to pur-
chase cattle, sheep, wine, or
other fermented drink.

Nehemiah 5:18 . . . . .Reference is made to an abundant supply of wine of all kinds.

Psalm 104:15 . . . . .Wine gladdens the heart of man.

Proverbs 3:9-10 . . . . .Honor the Lord with your
wealth. Then your barns will
fill to overflowing and your vats
will brim over with new wine.

Proverbs 20:1 . . . . .Wine is a mocker and beer is a
brawler. Whoever is led astray
by them is not wise.

Ecclesiastes 9:7 . . . . .Eat your food with gladness and
drink your wine with a joyful
heart.

Isaiah 28:7-8 . . . . .Priests and prophets stagger
from beer and are befuddled
with Wine.

Nahum 1:10 . . . . .Reference to Nineveh—they will
be entangled in thorns and drunk
from their wine.

Matthew 26:29 . . . . .Jesus says, "I will not drink of
this fruit of the vine until that
day when I drink it anew with
you in my Father's kingdom."

John 2:6-11 . . . . .Jesus turns water into wine. This
is His first miracle in Cana of
Galilee.

Ephesians 5:18 . . . . .Do not get drunk with wine,
which leads to debauchery.

1 Timothy 5:23 . . . . .Stop drinking only water. Use a little wine, because of your stomach problems and frequent illnesses.

WISDOM

1 Kings 3:16-28 . . . . .Two prostitutes argue over which one is the mother of the surviving child. King Solomon devises a test to determine who is the real mother.

Nehemiah 9:7-37 . . . . . . .Nehemiah explains to the Hebrews about God's goodness and the history of dealing with their sin (good short course of God helping the Israelites).

Job 28:12-28 . . . . .Man does not know where wisdom can be found. God alone knows where it can be found.

Job 37:7 . . . . .God stops every man from his labor so he may know God's work.

Psalm 111:10 . . . . .The fear of the Lord is the beginning of wisdom.

Psalm 139:4 . . . . .The Lord knows what we are going to say before we do.

Proverbs 2:6 . . . . .The Lord gives wisdom and from His mouth come knowledge and understanding.

Proverbs 11:30 . . . . .He who wins souls is wise.

Proverbs 24:27 . . . . .Build your house after you fin-
ish your outdoor work and
everything is ready in the field.

Proverbs 25:9-10, 17 . . . .Do not betray another man's
confidence. You will never lose
your bad reputation. Seldom set
foot in your neighbor's house.
He will hate you, so do not
become a nuisance.

Ecclesiastes 2:26 . . . . . . .Pleasures are meaningless to the
man who pleases Him. God
gives wisdom, knowledge, and
happiness. To the sinner He
gives the task of gathering and
storing up wealth to hand over
to the one whom God pleases.
This too is meaningless, a chasing after the wind.

Ecclesiastes 7:1 . . . . .The day of death is better than
the day of birth.

Ecclesiastes 7:3 . . . . .Sorrow is better than laughter,
because a sad face is good for
the heart.

Ecclesiastes 7:4 . . . . .The heart of the wise is in the
house of mourning, but the heart
of fools is in the house of
pleasure.

Ecclesiastes 7:18 . . . . . . .The man who fears God will
avoid all extremes.

Acts 7:10 . . . . .God gives Joseph wisdom and
enables him to gain the good
will of Pharaoh, King of Egypt.

Acts 7:22 . . . . .Moses is educated in all the wisdom of the Egyptians.

Romans 1:21-22 . . . . . . .Although they know God, they neither glorify him as God nor give thanks to him, but their thinking becomes futile, and their foolish hearts are darkened. They claim to be wise but become fools.

1 Corinthians 1:27 . . . . . .God chooses the foolish things of this world to shame the wise.

Hebrews 4:12-13 . . . . . . .God knows everything about us.

WITNESSING

Psalm 96:2 . . . . .Proclaim the Lord's salvation every day.

Ecclesiastes 11:1 . . . . . . .Cast your bread upon the waters, for after many days you will find it again.

Ezekiel 3:18-19 . . . . .Witness to wicked people, otherwise you will be held accountable.

Matthew 26:31-35, 69-75 . .Peter disowns Jesus three times (see Mark 14:27-31).

Matthew 28:19-20 . . . . . .The Great Commission is to go and make disciples of all the nations by baptizing them in the name of the Father, Son, and the Holy Spirit.

Mark 16:15-16 . . . . .Jesus says, "Go into all the world and preach the good news

to all creation. Whoever believes
and is baptized will be saved,
but whoever does not believe
will be condemned."

Luke 5:1-11 . . . . .Jesus changes the fishermen to
fishers of men. They pull their
boats up on shore, leave everything, and follow Jesus.

Luke 10:2 . . . . .The spiritual harvest of people
who need to be won to Christ is
plentiful, but the workers are few.

Luke 12:8-10 . . . . .Jesus will acknowledge you
before the angels of God if you
publicly acknowledge Him here
on earth. But he who disowns
Jesus publicly will be disowned
before the angels of God.

John 8:42-47 . . . . .Believe in God, not Satan, who
is the father of lies.

John 21:16-18 . . . . .Jesus says to Peter, "Take care
of my sheep."

Acts 1:7-8 . . . . .Jesus tells his apostles that they
will receive power from the
Holy Spirit. and they will be His
witnesses in Jerusalem, and in
all Judea and Samaria, and to
the ends of the earth.

Acts 4:8-12 . . . . .The apostle Peter is filled with
the Holy Spirit and speaks
before the Sanhedrin, proclaim-
ing Jesus Christ and reminding
them that they crucified Jesus
who gives salvation.

Romans 11:13 . . . . .The apostle Paul is God's spiritual messenger to the Gentiles.

2 Corinthians 4:3-6 . . . . .The god of this age (Satan) has
blinded the minds of unbelievers
so they cannot see the light of
the gospel of the glory of Christ.

2 Timothy 1:8 . . . . .Do not be ashamed to testify
about our Lord.

2 Timothy 3:16-17 . . . . . .All Scripture is God-breathed
and good for teaching, rebuking,
correcting, and training in righteousness, so that the man of
God may be thoroughly
equipped for every good work.

WOMEN

Genesis 2:21-23 . . . . .God makes woman from Adam's
rib.

Genesis 3:6 . . . . .Woman (Eve) eats first from the
tree of knowledge of good and
evil (see Genesis 2:17).

Genesis 3:15 . . . . .God puts hostility between
Satan and women for eating the
forbidden fruit.

Genesis 3:16 . . . . .God will greatly increase
women's childbearing pain for
eating the forbidden fruit. Man
will rule over woman.

Deuteronomy 22:5 . . . . . .A woman must not wear men's
clothing, nor a man wear
women's clothing.

Proverbs 11:22 . . . . .A beautiful woman who shows
no discretion is like a gold ring
in a pig's snout.

Proverbs 21:19 . . . . .It is better to live in a desert
than with a quarrelsome and ill-
tempered wife.

Proverbs 27:15-16 . . . . . .A quarrelsome wife is like a
constant dripping on a rainy day.
Restraining her is like restraining the wind or grasping oil with
the hand.

Luke 1:26-28 . . . . .God sends the angel Gabriel to
Nazareth who says to Mary,
"Greetings, you are highly
favored! The Lord is with you."

Luke 8:1-3 . . . . .Women of means help support
Jesus and the apostles (verse 3).

1 Corinthians 14:33-35 . .Women should remain silent in
church.

2 Corinthians 11:3 . . . . . .Eve is deceived by Satan's
cunning.

Galatians 3:28 . . . . .There is neither male or female
in Christ.

Ephesians 5:22-24 . . . . . .Wives, submit to your husbands
as to the Lord. For the husband
is the head of the wife as Christ
is head of the church.

1 Timothy 2:9-10 . . . . . . .Women should dress modestly
and with decency.

1 Timothy 2:11-15 . . . . . .A woman is not permitted to
teach or have authority over a

man. This is because Eve is the one deceived in the Garden of Eden, not Adam.

1 Timothy 5:9 . . . . No widow may be put on the widows' list unless she is over sixty years old and has been faithful to her husband.

WORLDLY POSSESSIONS

Psalm 49:1-20 . . . . There is not enough earthly wealth in the world to save one soul.

Psalm 52:7 . . . . Wicked men do not make God their stronghold, but trust in their wealth and grow stronger by destroying others.

Psalm 55:21 . . . . The wicked have speech as smooth as butter, yet war is in their heart. Their words are more soothing than oil, yet they are drawn swords.

Psalm 127:2 . . . . It is senseless to work from early morning to late at night.

Jeremiah 17:5-6 . . . . Cursed is the one who trusts in man, depends on flesh for his strength, and whose heart turns away from the Lord.

Jeremiah 22:13-15 . . . . . . A beautiful palace built by an unrighteous man does not make him a king.

plunge you into ruin and destruction.

1 Timothy 6:10 . . . . The love of money is a root of all kinds of evil.

1 Timothy 6:17-19 . . . . . . Command the rich to do good, to be rich in good deeds and not arrogant, to put their hope not in uncertain wealth but in God.

1 John 2:15-17 . . . . Do not love the world or anything in it. The ways of the world will pass away, but God's ways will live forever.

1 John 3:11-18 . . . . We should love one another. Do not be surprised if the world hates you. Anyone who hates another person is a murderer, and no murderer has eternal life in him.

The Road to Eternity

If you are looking for just a few important verses to witness to a friend or stranger or to strengthen your faith in Christ, these verses provide biblical truths that expose us to the wonderful gift of *salvation* through Jesus Christ.

Are you saved? Are you going to heaven? Will you have eternal life?

Matthew 10:32-33 . . . . . .Disown Jesus before men, and He will disown you.

Matthew 12:30 . . . . .Anyone not for Jesus is against Him.

John 3:18 . . . . .Whoever does not believe in Jesus stands condemned.

John 3:36 . . . . .Whoever rejects Jesus will not see eternal life.

Sinful behavior will prevent us from receiving eternal life and the glories of heaven.

1 Corinthians 6:9-11 . . . .Neither the sexually immoral nor idolaters, adulterers, male prostitutes, homosexuals, thieves, the greedy, drunkards, slanderers nor swindlers will enter heaven.

Galatians 5:19-21 . . . . . .People with a sinful nature or the sexually immoral, etc., will not enter heaven.

2 Thessalonians 1:8-9 . . .God will punish with everlasting destruction those who do not know and obey the gospel of our Lord Jesus.

Revelation 21:8 . . . . .The cowardly, the unbelieving, the vile, the murders, the sexually immoral, those who practice magical arts, the idolaters, and all liars will be in the fiery lake of burning sulfur (hell).

Repentance is mandated if we are to be "born again" and enjoy eternal life and heaven with Jesus.

2 Chronicles 7:14 . . . . . .Pray, seek God, and repent, and God will heal our land.

Jeremiah 15:19-21 . . . . . .God will save those who repent and change their ways.

Luke 13:3 . . . . .Jesus says, "Repent or perish."

John 15:19-21 . . . . .Do not belong to the world that persecuted Jesus and will persecute you also.

Acts 3:19 . . . . .Repent so that your sins may be wiped out.

Acts 17:30 . . . . .God commands all people everywhere to repent.

Believing, accepting, and following Jesus Christ as our Savior is the *only* road to salvation, eternal life, and heaven.

John 3:3 . . . . .You must be born again (spiritually) to enter heaven.

John 3:16 . . . . .Whoever believes in Jesus shall not
perish but have eternal life.

John 5:22 . . . . .God judges no one. Jesus will
judge everyone.

John 14:6 . . . . .No one comes to the Father except
through Jesus.

Acts 4:12 . . . . .Salvation is found in no one else
but Jesus.

Romans 10:9-13. . . . . .If you confess with your mouth that
Jesus is Lord and believe in your
heart that God raised Him from the
dead, you will be saved.

Revelation 1:18 . . . . .Jesus holds the keys of death and
hades (hell).

Turn to Jesus and *sincerely* pray, "Lord Jesus come into my heart and save me." God will give you a new life at that moment. Then repent of your sins and live a Christian life.